can i get there from here?

RUSTY WILLIAMS

can i get there from here?

one cop's irreverent look at faith

TATE PUBLISHING & *Enterprises*

Can I Get There From Here?
Copyright © 2009 by Rusty Williams. All rights reserved.

The opinions expressed by the author are not necessarily those of Tate Publishing, LLC.

Published by Tate Publishing & Enterprises, LLC
127 E. Trade Center Terrace | Mustang, Oklahoma 73064 USA
1.888.361.9473 | www.tatepublishing.com

Tate Publishing is committed to excellence in the publishing industry. The company reflects the philosophy established by the founders, based on Psalm 68:11,
"The Lord gave the word and great was the company of those who published it."

Book design copyright © 2009 by Tate Publishing, LLC. All rights reserved.
Cover design by Kellie Southerland
Interior design by Nathan Harmony

Published in the United States of America

ISBN: 978-1-60696-148-3
1. Autobiography
2. Religious: Christian
09.03.27

To my children,
Matt and Corey.
Your love, support, and encouragement amaze me every day.
You two give me more smiles and make me more proud than any father deserves.

———————————

For my angel.

You're the one who had faith in me and who never gave up on me.

Your countless hours of reading, correcting, rereading, and proofing, as well as your unending encouragement and love have given me all that I need.

Elissa, you are a gift.

———————————————

acknowledgments

The author wishes to express his gratitude to those who have made this book possible:

The men and women who make up the best police department in the world: you've had my back more times than I can recall; and you've forged a path lined with integrity, honor and respect. To you, the members of the Medford Township Police Department, I say thank you.

The faculty and staff at Shawnee High School: you have given me all the support, encouragement and inspiration anyone could ever ask. Thank you for teaching me—about life.

Rob Rinier, my proofreader: your suggestions, time, and patience will always be remembered. Thank you, my friend.

The Cafeteria Ladies–Diane, Rose and Dawn: the readers of the first draft of this book. Thank you for your time and praise for the book—they kept me going until it was finished.

Raina DiMarco–librarian, media specialist and just all-round great person. Thank you for your energy and tenacity in seeing this through. You believed in this and for that I am grateful.

My brother Glenn and his wife, Nancy, and my nephews Drew and Anthony: thanks for being the best family a brother, brother-in-law, and uncle could want.

The many colleagues, friends and family who were there for me during some not-so-good times—I can never repay you, but I can thank you. You know who you are and I will never forget each of you being there for me.

The congregation, ministers and staff of a little church in Medford Lakes, The Protestant Community Church: words cannot describe my heartfelt thanks for welcoming us and for your openness, kindness, and genuine friendliness that brought me back to everything that is important in life.

And finally to the staff at Tate Publishing: you took a chance on me. Thank you for your faith in this book.

foreword

This is a very *powerful* book. It is *powerfully* insightful, *powerfully* funny, *powerfully* informative, but mostly *powerfully* inspirational. Rusty has managed to cover an incredible amount of very deeply spiritual and religious concepts in such a down to earth, easy to read manner I could not wait to turn the pages.

Rusty writes with tremendous wisdom but does not preach. He presents the material with so much humility and fun that anyone who reads the book is entertained while digesting very profound ideas for their consideration. The book is so fundamentally vulnerable in its presentation that it reads like a front porch conversation with a sage who does not act like he knows it all.

I loved Rusty's humor. He reveals his own humanness while penning a book about the glory of God. His own deep convictions are offered to the reader without the accompanying "I know God better than you" kind of lecture that turns people off. Although he provides powerful academic credence to all his points, he allows the reader the space to experience the information and learn from it in a very personal manner.

You see, Rusty has managed to pique the interest of those who profoundly believe in all the power of God's loving nature, to readers who may be searching, and to those who are lost; that is a talent for sure. I truly feel even an atheist could read this book and get some serious food for thought and consideration.

What I enjoyed most about "Can I Get There From Here?" is that Rusty gives you the opportunity to experience and increase your own level of spirituality. The tenets of this book can be the fuel to skyrocket your dreams to new heights. As you turn the pages of this treasure you will uncover the miracles of Rusty's life. He writes about those miracles in a way that makes the reader excited about the possibilities in their own life, especially when one is connected to the one true source, God. You will be unable to help yourself while reading this great book; you *WILL* reconnect to your own passion.

This book really presents you with a choice right now to take the first step and commit yourself to the knowing that something greater than your own ego is guiding the way. By reading this book, you have a tremendous opportunity right in front of you–right now. Today is your chance to decide to go on this journey with Rusty.

Allow him to take you deep within his stories as a mechanism to recall yours and perhaps discover what he has discovered. God loves us and God wants us to be glorious expressions of all that is good; to make a contribution to the world like Rusty has done and continues to do; to recognize your miracles and look out for your angels as they present themselves. They are always there in one form or another. Just ask Rusty.

I am a better person because I have read this book, you will be too!

God Bless,
Kevin M. Touhey
Best Selling Author
The Miracle of Optimism

table of contents

who's this about?

Of all the things that are hard to explain and even harder to hold on to, *faith* has to be up there in the top ten. It's certainly something that gets people talking—sometimes arguing. Yep, my *faith* is better than yours; I have more *faith* than you do; here's the right way to have *faith*. Everyone seems to be an expert in something, and when the subject of faith comes along, so many are happy to give you their opinion.

My hope, as you read the following pages, is that together we are able to open a dialog about faith. Some of us have unshakable faith; some of us have faith—but with concerns; others have questioned their own faith; while still more might be at a point where they've lost their faith.

Wherever you are on this road of life, this book is meant to look at faith in a way that just might make sense to you—and me! Maybe if it's (faith) not jammed down our throats we'll be more apt to look at it with an open mind. And that's what you'll find in the pages that follow—a discussion on faith that's not shoved down your throat. But with faith comes questions.

Here are some questions you, the reader, must be asking yourself:

So what's the purpose of this book?

Why did you write it?

And what credentials do you have to write something like this?

Who do you think you are?

How many other questions do you have? Go ahead, insert any additional questions you might have here; I'll wait ...

Here's one I have: have you ever needed to see something in the dark, grabbed a flashlight and tried to turn it on—only to find out it didn't work? Just wondering.

So many questions, so few answers! Does that sound like your life? All questions and very few, if any, answers? It sounded like mine—for a long time.

As I write this, I'm nearing the end of my career as a police officer. More than two decades in the cop business has definitely taken its toll on me. The toll it has taken is both physical and spiritual. All the research available shows that cops die way before their counterparts in other professions. Probably because of the constant state of awareness cops are in, we can never let our guard down—even when we're off duty (ask the family member of a cop if he or she is ever *off duty*). The adrenaline that is constantly being pumped into our bloodstream apparently takes its toll on the body. Add to that the shift work and the junk we eat on night watch, and you've got a recipe (attempted pun intentional) for disaster. Feel free to insert any cop/donut joke you want here ...

As far as the spiritual carnage: how much death and suffering can a person see before it affects him? The things seen and experienced by a cop would make anyone question aspects of life. Especially God! And the ruthlessness, callousness, brutality, and violence witnessed each and every day make cops wonder about humanity and ask: "Why does God allow these things to happen to innocent people?" Even working in the sleepy town where I've spent the last twenty-two years on the job, I've been part of some gruesome and heart-wrenching events. Hey, while I'm on the subject of me (not much longer, I promise), let me add that before I was a cop, I was a paramedic in, what was at that time (the early 1980s), the most violent and poorest city in America. Boy, do I have some stories from those days ...

I still wake up screaming with vivid dreams (nightmares if you will) of the children who I couldn't save—both as a cop and as a paramedic. Their faces and the looks of terror and/or innocence are still as fresh today as they were when they happened all those years ago. Nothing a few doses of self-prescribed alcohol couldn't take care of to dull the pain. The pain's gone, but the images still remain.

And continuing to rewind the clock just a bit more, I was going to become an Episcopal priest before being accepted into the paramedic program. One semester at Rutgers studying sociology and religion, then I broke my mother's heart. I quit college to become a paramedic. No degree, no pomp and circumstance; just a license by the State of New Jersey to treat the sick and injured. Don't get me wrong, my mom was proud as hell of me and told all her friends, coworkers, and relatives of my career choice. She even bought a scanner to listen to the emergency calls. She was proud of me, as was my father, but I still think I disappointed her when I left Rutgers. Okay, I might as well be honest: I left Rutgers before I got kicked out. Passing one class out of four wasn't going to cut it anyway; know what I mean?

And before college, there was high school. Anyone remember that? Yeah, I think we're in the same boat. The only thing I'll share with you (my kids just might end up reading this, and I haven't told them *everything* yet) is that my high school career started with me getting suspended the first week of my freshman year. My choices and decisions didn't get much better the next three years as I got to know my disciplinarian very well! But by the end of my junior year, I think I got it figured out and actually found Christ on a youth retreat weekend that I went on to meet girls (the Lord *definitely* works in mysterious ways). I calmed down and started enjoying life; more importantly, I found some meaning to life. I became active in our church youth group and became a youth leader. So by my senior year I went from a freak to a Jesus freak—almost overnight. And it was during my senior year that I decided to become a priest.

I don't know why my path changed from priesthood to paramedic. It just felt like the right thing to do. Just like writing this book—it just seems like the right thing to do. I can't explain it any better than that. And speaking of explaining, one more thing needs to be explained so you understand me a little better and maybe get some of your questions answered. After four years as a paramedic, I knew it was time for a change. Not that I didn't enjoy it, but I knew I was burned out. I thought police work might be something interesting, as it was still helping people. Yep, that's what I told the township manager and the police chief during my interview: I wanted to become a police officer to help people. And besides, I rationalized that if I was going to get shot at while I was at work (remember I was in the poorest and most violent city in America), then I might as well take a job where I could shoot back!

During my years as a paramedic, my mother was diagnosed with breast cancer. A year later, my father was diagnosed with lung cancer. My mother had a mastectomy, radiation, and chemotherapy and at first appeared to have beaten it. My father was getting radiation and chemotherapy and seemed to be on his way to being cured. The months went on, and I told my mom that I was going to become a cop—she had a look of sheer panic on her face and in her voice. My dad was his usual stoic, yet proud and determined self. He told me, and I'll always remember this, that if you find something you love doing it will never be work.

My mom's condition worsened, but my father's improved. Each and every night I'd pray like there was no tomorrow. I'd pray for a miracle, even though the medical side of me had to know it wasn't going to happen. But I prayed every chance I had. Not for *me*, but for *them*—especially my mom. I thought that since I had this great relationship with God, he'd answer my prayers and that would be all there was to it. The harder I prayed the sicker she got. The last thing she

can i get there from here?

made me promise her was that if I got hired as a police officer, I would always wear my bulletproof vest. I promised her
that I would, and to this day, regardless of the temperature, I
have worn my vest whenever the uniform is on, as well as the
few times working plainclothes details.

By the way, they're really not "bulletproof" vests; we call
them ballistic soft body armor. Sounds a lot more macho that
way, don't you think? Actually, they're not bullet-proof because
they aren't meant to stop every type of round that can be fired
at you. If cops wore vests that were literally bullet-proof,
they wouldn't be able to chase the bad guys on foot, let alone
scratch their back. For those of you that don't know what I'm
talking about—there's *nothing* worse than having an itch in
the middle of your back when you're wearing a vest! Okay, I
got off track, where was I? Oh yeah, my mom. I got the word
that I was hired and would start in two weeks, and by then my
mom was basically in a coma lying in a nursing home.

My first day on the job came and I was assigned to day-
watch, 8 a.m. to 4 p.m.. I got home around 4:30 to the sound
of the phone ringing (the phone on the wall in the kitchen,
no cell phones back then). I answered it, and it was my dad.
He told me to get to the nursing home as soon as possible;
they couldn't get a blood pressure on my mom. I called my
brother's work and told him to meet us at the nursing home.
I got there just in time to watch my father hold his wife for
the last time; I watched life leave her body and she died. I
immediately went into *paramedic mode*—clinical and techni-
cal instead of emotional. I tried to figure out which of her
organs failed; in what order did they quit? My dad kept asking my mom the rhetorical question: "Why did the chemo

work for me and not you?" That was repeated through his tears until we left together as a family.

That was in late September. By the following spring, my dad's cancer had returned. His odds were a lot steeper than my mom's, with respect to beating "the bug," as he called it. And he knew it. I drove him to chemo and he would throw-up on the way there, just thinking about it. I watched as he lost weight over the summer and then started to wither away as the cancer spread to his liver. As anyone who knows anything about cancer can tell you, once it hits the liver, you're basically screwed. The weekend before Thanksgiving, my dad went into the hospital. It would be his last visit.

I woke up Thanksgiving morning to the sound of the phone ringing (here comes more good news—part II). The nurse said my dad died in the middle of the night. I wasn't even there to say goodbye. Just like that I was an orphan at the ripe old age of 25, my brother an orphan at 24. And on Thanksgiving morning...

Thanks, God, just wonderful!

That was the nicest thing I said to him in the days and nights that followed. Wanna hear what else I said to him? Okay, since you want to know: Besides the usual "I hate you," and "how could you do this," I actually told him to go have sex with himself. Yep, I told the Big Guy to... well... you know. Not only that, I told him to leave me alone; I didn't want him or need him in my life. I was going to handle life on my own! After all, how could he do this? Both of my parents were active in their church; mom was on the altar guild and dad was a lay reader. In addition to that, dad was in the Masonic Lodge and mom was in Eastern Star. I mean, how much better people could you ask for to be saved? And what about me? I spent the last four years helping others as a paramedic; on a salary that barely made ends meet. I viewed my parents as righteous and me as doing righteous things for others. If anyone deserved to have his prayers answered it was me, damn it! And if there were ever any two people who deserved to be prayed for, it was my parents. But what does he do? He lets them die. And their deaths weren't without misery, and pain, and embarrassment, and discomfort, and ... and ...

So after they were both dead and buried, I set out on my own. What good was he anyway? I could do this thing called life just as good as he could, and I certainly wouldn't hurt anyone in the process. And I would *definitely* answer someone's call for help, their prayer if you will, without thinking twice about it. Screw him, screw religion, and screw my faith; in fact, screw everyone!

So what do you think of me now? I had you feeling sorry for me there for a while, didn't I? Then, blam! It hits you, like being smacked in the face. I can hear some of you now: "Such a nice young man, he wanted to become a priest, then he became a paramedic, and finally a police officer. For his mother to die on the day he started as a police officer and his father to die the following Thanksgiving morning, what a shame. He went through a lot, and at such a young age ..." Then the sucker punch gets delivered, "He said *what* to God?!" "He told God to go do *what*?!"

I tell you these things not looking for sympathy and certainly not to wear as a badge of courage. And I ask that you don't judge me, not just yet. Yes this is about me. But who else is it about? Is it about you? How about the other guy?

And what about you, the one shaking her head? I'm not for one second suggesting that anyone who has read this far has said these things or had these thoughts. However, have you ever been so mad at God that you just wanted to scream? How many times did you want to let him know just how disappointed you were in your unanswered prayers? And how many times did you question your own faith? You see, I gave you a glimpse of my life to answer some of the questions you had at the outset. You remember, the ones on the first page. Go ahead, go back and read them, I'll wait (like I have anything better to do right now anyway). See the ones about my credentials; why did I write this book; and who do I think I am? Hey, you were thinking them in the first place; all I did was write them down. Now that you have an idea about me, do you want to read any further?

And by the way, if you haven't actually bought this book yet but are sitting in some book store, sipping a latte, skimming through it to see if you like it—please buy the thing! I have kids to put through college, and there's no way I'm gonna be able to do that on a cop's pension! So go ahead, take it to the cashier and put a couple of bucks down, I'll wait (again).

If you've gotten this far, chances are you're interested, or at least curious, in just where the hell I'm going with this. Perhaps you saw the cover, found it interesting, and took it home to read. As you can see, and more will become evident as you read on, the only credentials I have to write a book is that maybe I'm a little bit like you. Maybe we're a lot alike, you and me. I don't have a degree, never took a writing course; however I have written hundreds, no make that thousands of police reports. Most importantly, I have questioned my faith—just like you. And in case you're wondering (don't skip to the last chapter!), my faith has been restored. It's been restored in a remarkable way through a remarkable woman. So it has a happy ending (no, not that you sicko!). Don't cheat and look at the last chapter to see who I'm referring to or what happened to restore it; just know that I have a faith that is stronger than ever; and that's thanks to an angel.

So here's the answer to the first question:

This is written for those who question, or have questioned, their faith—in other words, for *all of us*!

But what's faith? Go ahead, Google it, I'll wait (there's definitely a pattern here). Regardless of what Mr. Google says, here's my definition: Faith can be described, or defined if you must, as *"Believing in something that can't be proven."* Here's the Wikipedia definition:

To commit one's self to act based on sufficient evidence to warrant belief, but without absolute proof.

Hey, I was pretty close, don't ya think? And while we're on the subject, as great as Wikipedia is, and as awesome as all the stuff on the Internet is, please take most of what you read out there with a grain of salt! Trust me on this. Hey, maybe even have *faith* in my suggestion (sometimes my own wit amazes me).

Just as important as knowing what this book is, you need to know what this book *is not*. It *is not* a theological study to prove the existence of God. I don't have the credentials, education, or patience for that. It *is not* a discussion of passages from the Bible to explain why faith is ours to use in order to get closer to God. See explanation above. And it *is not* a historical journey through the books of the Bible to find our faith together. If you're looking for that, try the self-help section in the book store. This is also *not a book* to get you to believe in God; belief and faith are two different things. This is not meant to be intimidating, deep, confusing or daunting. You've got better things to do with your time, and to be honest, I couldn't think of any more stuff to add to make this book any thicker. As a paramedic, the cardiologist who lectured on the heart had a philosophy of imparting his knowledge to us. It was the KISS principle, and I've been using it ever since. If you don't know what the KISS principle is, go ahead and Google it ... yeah, I'll wait.

Hey, just a heads-up. If you notice any typos in this chapter it's not my fault. There's a cat walking across the keyboard and he won't leave me alone. His name is Bojangles, and he's cute, but right now he's being a pain in the butt. Just a little too affectionate—he keeps nudging my arm to pet him and he won't stop. Come on, cat, leave me alone! Oh no, I think I hurt his feelings, now he won't come near me. I'm sorry, come here ...

All right, he's back on my lap, let's hope for the best. Hey, no jokes about a cat on my lap, that's too easy! But you know what I've been thinking that's *not* going to be easy? How am I going to get this book published? I got no idea where to take this? Here I go, setting off on a venture (which by the way I have *no* idea where or how it's going to end), and I have to hope that someone who reads it likes it and wants to take a chance on me. Sometimes ya just gotta have faith, know what I mean?

Let me know if you have any suggestions on how to get published. On second thought, that's not gonna work either, because if you're reading this, that means that it already got published. Great, where were you when I needed you?

Have you ever felt like that and asked: "Where were *you* when I needed you?" Me too.

Hey, today is Friday (as I'm writing this page); what day of the week is it for you right now? Just something to think about. Especially if it's Friday where you are. What do you think the chances are that you're reading this paragraph on a foggy Friday morning (8:40 EST to be exact)? Now that would be something!

I guess we have to get started—or else this'll never get published!

The hypothesis of this book is simple: By answering a few basic questions, and some additional, more thought-provoking questions, one can come to an understanding that faith doesn't have to be complicated but is there waiting for us to grab. In fact, God made it so that it wouldn't be complicated—he knows we're not all rocket scientists!

The questions that follow are meant to be simple on face value; but we'll look into them more in-depth starting with the first question—the *big* question: Is there a God?

So, we start our journey with the one topic that has both brought people together and torn them apart. First, though, you must promise yourself the following as you read this book: There's no need to worry (he'll do it for us), no need to try to figure everything out (he's knows we're not rocket scientists, remember?), and there's no need to think faith is an all or nothing thing (he knows we have questions).

Deal? Okay, here goes.

Let's start with the basic yes or no questions.

––––––––––––––

My bad. Sorry, I wanted to start off with something spiritual that might jump out at someone—to somehow get this started off with a prayer. Kinda like saying grace before dinner. So I added this prayer that first got me thinking about God when I was a senior in high school. I know there's some disagreement on its origin and purpose, but I think it'll fit nicely here and serve as a reminder for the remainder of the book.

Desiderata

Go placidly amid the noise and haste,
and remember what peace there may be in silence.
As far as possible, without surrender, be
on good terms with all persons.
Speak your truth quietly and clearly; and listen to others,
even the dull and the ignorant; they too have their story.

Avoid loud and aggressive persons, they
are vexations to the spirit.
If you compare yourself with others, you may become vain and bitter;
for always there will be greater and lesser persons than yourself.

Enjoy your achievements as well as your plans.
Keep interested in your own career, however humble;
it is a real possession in the changing fortunes of time.

Exercise caution in your business affairs;
for the world is full of trickery.
But let this not blind you to what virtue there is;
many persons strive for high ideals;
and everywhere life is full of heroism.

Be yourself.
Especially, do not feign affection.
Neither be cynical about love;
for in the face of all aridity and disenchantment
it is as perennial as the grass.

Take kindly the counsel of the years,
gracefully surrendering the things of youth.
Nurture strength of spirit to shield you in sudden misfortune.
But do not distress yourself with dark imaginings.
Many fears are born of fatigue and loneliness.

Beyond a wholesome discipline, be gentle with yourself.
You are a child of the universe, no less
than the trees and the stars;
you have a right to be here.
And whether or not it is clear to you,
no doubt the universe is unfolding as it should.

Therefore be at peace with God,
whatever you conceive him to be,
and whatever your labors and aspirations,
in the noisy confusion of life keep peace with your soul.
With all its sham, drudgery, and broken dreams,
it is still a beautiful world.
Be cheerful.
Strive to be happy.

—Anonymous

can i get there from here?

is there a god?

Most of us (we're not going to take on the atheists here—
that's another book for another time) would answer this
question as *Yes*. Yes, there is a God. Although we won't all
agree on who he is, what he does, and why he does it, most
of us would agree that there is a God. A God that at times
seems to contradict himself; a God that we hope loves us,
and at the same time, a God that we fear. Most of us would
agree that when we look around at all the stuff in the world
there has to be something greater than us at work. Call it a
higher power, call it something that can't be explained, call
it whatever you want; most of us—even the most cynical
thinkers—believe in *something* greater than us.

And what about our universe? Think about it. It has a
definite order to it, doesn't it? And what about our beloved
planet, called Earth? The only planet in our solar system
that can sustain life. So how many planets are there? Besides

can i get there from here?

being a troublemaker in school, I was also a lousy student, so I gotta go check this out. I'll be right back.

Got it. There are nine planets in our solar system; unless you count the new one, the one past Pluto (2003 UB313), then you got ten. I think Pluto got canned a couple of years ago, so we're back to nine. Nine or ten; the Internet says nine, so we'll stick with that. Pretty good for a kid who spent most of his high school career in the principal's office.

Ah man, now I found another reference that talks about "the Kuiper belt." How do you pronounce that anyway? Is it *Koo-eh-per*, *Ku-I-per*, *Koo-ip-er* ... Now I'm confused. Wanna join me in the confusion? Check out this text regarding the possibility of additional planets in our solar system I found at www.gps.caltech.edu:

> *If we assume that the typical small Kuiper belt object reflects 10% of the sunlight that hits its surface we know how bright a 400 km object would be in the Kuiper belt. As of late August 2006, 44 objects this size or larger in the Kuiper belt (including, of course, 2003 UB313 and Pluto), and one (Sedna) in the region beyond the Kuiper belt. In addition our large ongoing Palomar survey has detected approximately 30 more objects of this size which are currently undergoing detailed study.*

So how many planets are there? Me either; no wonder our kids are so confused. When I went to school, I got the wire coat hangers from my dad's closet, painted some Styrofoam balls and stuck them into the ends of the coat hangers. The biggest ball was the sun and the other *Nine* balls were the planets. By the way, Chinette paper plates held up the best for the rings around Saturn—in case you have to help your kids with their science fair project.

And while we're on that subject, how many of you have ever been to one of those elementary school science fairs? Am I the only one that got pissed off because I made my kid do the project *himself*? Of course I was there to help him, but he painted the planets and arranged them himself. He even got his penlight and stuck it in the sun to show how the shadow of the earth hits the moon. But when I walked around and saw some of the other projects...The Franklin Institute doesn't have the technology that some of these had! I think NASA engineers attached their resumes to some of them. Come on, parents, let your kids be kids! How are they supposed to learn if you (or your friends who work for the aerospace industry) do your kids' work? We can only hope that our kids' teachers see their work for what it is—*their* work. Okay, I'm off my soap box now, where was I?

Can we agree, for the sake of argument, that we have nine planets in our solar system? If you're a science teacher and want to argue this, please don't e-mail me unless you attach a funny/dirty joke to your comments. Thank you.

Okay, if there are nine planets and one sun (another subject for debate from the scholars out there), that means that the chances of our planet (Earth) being the only one able to sustain life is...I hated math, but I think I can figure this one out without any help...One out of nine or eleven percent (my math teachers' faces have just lit up). So we had a little better than a ten percent chance that Earth would be the one planet capable of sustaining life. If you were given the chance to invest all of your money in a mutual fund that

can i get there from here?

had a ten percent chance of making money, would you do it? Just trying to put things into perspective, because you'd have a ninety percent chance of losing everything with that financial advisor. How about a ten percent chance in some surgical procedure? Okay, a ten percent chance of taking off and landing safely at your destination? Hey, I'm all for taking risks, but if you're only giving me a ten percent chance of things turning out in my favor, forget about it.

So we're sitting on this rock in space (the only rock where we could survive) and it has just the right amount of oxygen, helium, nitrogen and other elements that our bodies need to live. Our rock is about ninety-three million miles away from the sun (give or take a couple of miles for the elliptical orbit we're in). That distance is exactly where the earth has to be positioned in order for us not to be in a constant state of ice or a constant state of molten lava. Of the nine planets that were dropped into position, what are the odds that this one would fall into just the right place so that we could go skiing in the mountains in winter and work on our tan in the summer? Dermatologists, please note: I use sun screen—SPF thirty to be exact! The earth's atmosphere is made up of different gases, twenty-one percent is oxygen—exactly what we need to live. What are the odds of that? One out of a hundred I guess. The rock we're on is tilted exactly twenty-three-and-a-half degrees with respect to its rotation around the sun. This tilt is exactly what the earth needs for the change of seasons, magnetic north, and the different climates, let alone for us not to fry or freeze to death. If it could be rotated 180 degrees in any direction, what are the odds that it just happened to stop at twenty-three-and-a-half degrees?

The makeup of our planet, or the land to water ratio, has been made for us to not only enjoy, but for us to flourish. Think about it, our planet is what, seventy percent water (same as our bodies)? That water has just the right amount of salt in it to help with the cleansing process of a lot of stuff, and to maintain life for the fish in it. (Before I forget—I know I'm not the only one who loves a nice Tuna steak, encrusted with cracked pepper and grilled until medium rare.) So all this water is there, in just the right quantity and quality to help with oxygen and other gasses, and climates, and weather. And don't forget the beaches!

If you could be dropped on a tropical beach anywhere in the world, where would it be? Have you ever watched a sunset on a beach? Talk about beauty! You just gotta ask yourself: how does that sun produce all those colors as it disappears under the horizon? Yeah, I know, there's some scientific explanation about dust particles, atmosphere and other meteorological conditions that create the reds, purples, pinks, and yellows. But come on, just for a minute, haven't you ever just thought, "Wow, how does he do it?"

If I were any smarter; and this is *no* reflection on my former math teachers (by the way, thank you Mrs. Williams, Mr. Gibney and Mr. Fisher), I'd be able to figure out what the odds or chances are that the earth's atmosphere, distance from the sun, tilt, and make-up (land-water ratio) would all be exactly what they are to make earth the only planet that we know of (for you UFO guys out there) that has life on it. Because if you take the odds of any one of them, it's at best a little better than ten percent shot. But when combined, if just one of those factors is off by as little as one percent, the whole thing's a bust. What would the odds be, like one out of three-hundred-thirty-six-thousand-billion-quadrillion or something like that? I don't know what it would be, but it (the odds—the ratio) would definitely be written as the number one with a colon after it followed by a really big number with a lot of commas in it. That's all I know (I think that was Algebra II, sorry if I disappointed you, Mr. Fisher).

It's just too much of a coincidence for me to think there was this big explosion billions of years ago and everything we just talked about happened to fall into just the right place, in just the right way and at just the right time. No, I think you'd agree with me on this (unless you're with the guy who'd jump on the plane with a ten percent chance of making it to your destination), somehow this whole thing was a well thought out process by someone who's a lot smarter than us. For the sake of argument, can we call him God?

So, we got over that hurdle—probably the most significant hurdle for us to get over in our quest for faith. And these questions are described as hurdles on purpose. They are there in front of us, each and every day. We can look at them (our questions, doubts, concerns) as roadblocks put there to screw-up our world, or they can be looked at as opportunities to conquer our doubts, answer our questions, and gain satisfaction over our concerns. Yes, hurdles can be intimidating when first looked at. But when we look at them as opportunities, they become chances for us to prove something to ourselves. Just as a sprinter at the starting line sees them as opportunities, so can we if we get into the right mind-set.

And we do say "getting over" the hurdles. We could ignore them and go around them, but where would the satisfaction be? No, instead we are going to go over them, knowing full well that God expects us to stumble. It's harder to go over a problem than to go around it, but that's the only way to get *real* satisfaction and *real* answers, and ultimately gain a *real* understanding from it.

So, we agree that there is a God; now let's move to the next question.

is he a loving god?

Ah, not as easy to answer as the first question! When you picture God, what do you see? An old man with a beard, perhaps holding a staff in his hand? Maybe it's an image of a being that only has a face, no body. Or perhaps it's not an image of a human, but of some life-like creature that only you know. Whatever image you have, does it hold love? In other words, is the God you picture capable of producing a feeling of love when you think of him? Even if fear and anxiety accompany your thoughts of your God, is there love in there somewhere? Once again, the overwhelming majority of us believe *our* God is a loving God. A God that while powerful and just, also loves us. And most of us have at one time or another said, "thank God," to something that has happened (or failed to happen). Have you ever thought about that? How many times have we used that phrase when something has happened to us or someone we love? Unfortunately, and I think you'd agree, we use that phrase as a "throw-away" type of line to emphasize

can i get there from here?

something we want to get across to someone. Well, if we've all said it, doesn't it just make sense that we're thanking him for something that we attribute to his love?

Yes, he can be (and *should* be) a feared God, an intimidating force in our lives that demands respect. He has done things to people and earth that leave many scratching their heads—Sodom and Gomorrah ring a bell? How about that guy named Noah and the task he was given when God was pissed with us again? Yes, it's a little—okay, *a lot*—scary when we think of his power and his wrath. But can't we also think of something that has happened in our past that shows how he demonstrated his love? We say we believe there is a God, as we did in the previous question, and we agree that *most* of us believe in a God. If we think of a God that only offers fear, anxiety and plagues, why do so many of us still believe in him? It seems to reason that his story (his legacy) couldn't have stood the test of time if all he offered was misery. No instead, he offers hope—hope of something better, something greater, something special—and that hope is built on love.

Go look up the science of love, Google it, and see what you find. You'll find explanations that include brain chemicals like Dopamine, Adrenaline, and Serotonin, hormones and brain function. But you can't find *why* or *how* love is what it is. Remember, there is a difference between the brain and the mind. Scientists think they're beginning to understand the brain, but we're no where close to understanding the mind. There are a lot of theories, but scientists still can't quantify it like they can solids, liquids and gas (remember 10th grade chemistry?). We'll talk more about this subject later, but for now, can we agree that love is something that is very hard to explain with scientific certainty?

Forget about science, how about something we can all relate to? How about if we use our imagination for a minute; this might be more real than imagined for some of us.

Here goes:

You have an entry-level job, making barely enough money to pay your bills. You're a junior account manager with a major firm on Wall Street, or Fifth Avenue if you want to be there (that should minimize any potential lawsuits or hate mail). Your financial future is hanging on the biggest negotiation you've ever been involved in. Your boss has hand-picked *you* to work this deal. You've devoted 14-hour days since last month, slept at the office the last two weekends and your relationship with your family has consisted of "good night" and "good morning" on your cell phone. The pressure has never been greater in your entire life, but the rewards will never be sweeter. Your boss is going to use this as a gauge to promote you to senior account manager, which means a big raise and a bonus. You'll be able to get caught up on your mortgage payments, car payments, and the back credit card bills. Finally, you'll be able to sleep at night without worrying where the money's going to come from; no more living paycheck-to-paycheck, no more financial worries!

It's the morning of the big meeting and you get up early to make sure you look your best. Best suit, best shirt, best shoes—you know the routine. The executive you are trying to sell to is a fanatic for appearance. From what you've heard, he's as anal retentive as they come, and looks mean *every-thing* to him. Other companies have lost deals with this guy because he didn't think their office was neat enough, or they didn't look professional, or the account manager looked like a slob. Oh, by the way, your boss could be this guy's cloned twin. No pressure, right?

As you wait in the lobby to meet Mr. Big Shot, you see your brother getting off the elevator. You haven't seen him in months and he happened to take the day off today and surprise you at work. And guess what, he brought your three-year-old nephew with him. Your godchild is coming off the elevator behind him. This little fellow is as rambunctious as they come and you two have this thing where he gets a running start and leaps into your arms whenever you meet.

When he sees you his eyes light up. And his smile, you love that little smile. As he shifts into third gear, about twenty feet from you, you notice he's carrying a half-eaten chocolate ice cream cone in his hand. The heat in your building has taken its toll on what's left of it, and most of that is all over your nephew's hands, wrists, arms, chin, cheeks, and shirt. You gradually begin to withdraw your outstretched arms as your stomach starts to churn and your mind switches to the meeting with Mr. Big Shot.

He's in fourth gear now, full speed ahead, and he's getting ready to leap into your arms; the arms of his godparent. His father, your brother, yells, "Hey, you better watch out, we just came from the park across the street and he was rolling on the grass and stomping in all the puddles." You look down to see he's covered in mud from his waist down. Whatever part of his little body isn't covered in chocolate is soaking wet with leaves and grass clippings and has mud dripping from it.

He's a foot from you now, his arms are outstretched in anticipation of your hug—his most favorite hug of all his relatives, even his own father. Yep, you two share a special bond that has every other member of the family jealous. The one thing you always made this little bundle of energy promise you was that he *always* had to give you a big hug *whenever* he saw you. He's definitely going to show you how much he loves you, and here's your chance to show him how much you love him.

Here's the question: What do you do?

Have you seen the movie *My Cousin Vinny*? Was that a great movie or what? Remember the scene where Vinny Gambini (Joe Pesci) and Mona Lisa Vito (Marisa Tomei) are staying at D.A. Trotter's cabin in the woods? The one where they fall asleep in the car during the rain storm and wake-up late the next morning to get to court. The car is stuck in the mud and Vinny gets out to push it. He slips in the mud and falls flat on his back; then he ends up rolling in the mud as he tries to get his footing. He opens up the trunk and flings his suit out and watches it land in the mud. It's the only suit he owns, and the only one Judge Chamberlain Haller III approves of. Ms. Vito thought she would surprise him, so she had the suit dry-cleaned for him. Then she laid it neatly in the back of the trunk so he would have it for his big court day. Can you imagine what was going through Vinny Gambini's head at that time? What a great scene, don't you think? Well, that's just my sense of humor, I guess. But you have to admit, it was pretty damn funny.

Okay, back on track; where were we? That little three-year-old running at his most favorite person in the whole wide world, that's where we were. And the question was, let me go back and check...

"What do you do?"

You don't have to answer; but think about this instead. What do you think God would do? Do you think he would draw back his arms as you sprinted to him? Do you think he would worry about the meeting and everything that was riding on it?

Wanna know what I think? I believe that at that very moment, the *only* thing that God would be thinking of is you! Nothing else would matter to him; you would be the only thing on his mind. And I'll bet you I'm right. He doesn't care what shape you're in, what condition your clothes are in; he knows you're going to make a mess when he wraps you in his arms. And he knows you're not going to know any better. After all, you were seeking him and wanted his love; you wanted to feel his presence. I don't think he would pull away, worrying about his suit, do you?

If you'll agree with me on that, can we agree that love just might be something that God gave us? Something that God gave us as his gift to us? If that's the case, then we answer *yes* to, "Is he a loving God?"

By the way, why can't they make a waffle cone that doesn't have a crack in the bottom of it? I find myself eating my vanilla-chocolate swirl soft serve so fast I get a headache. But if I don't eat it really fast, the thing starts to leak all down the front of me. And if I wrap it in a napkin, then I end up eating paper because the damn napkin sticks to the cone. If you're in the ice cream business, please try to get this problem *ironed* out by next summer. Thank you.

(Waffle *iron*, get it? Go ahead and add ten points if you thought that was clever.)

Remember the game show from the 70s, *Let's Make A*

Deal? You show up wearing your craziest-looking Christian outfit, hoping to be picked. You brought with you your faith in God; his love. You jumped up and down enough to get noticed, and after the commercial break, Monty Hall comes your way. He sees that you have the love of God in your hand. But this is Let's Make A Deal, and you're here to get the *best* deal. The television cameras are on you as Monty reads your name tag and makes mention of your costume—a Christian.

What if Monty Hall asked you if you wanted what was behind door number one, door number two, or door number three? You know that there's a ton of money behind one of the doors—maybe behind door number two. And there are also cars, entertainment systems, trips, and other amenities—perhaps behind door number three. And there's a chance of eternal damnation behind one of the doors. You have an absolute known possession in the palm of your hand. All you're asked to do is give up what's in your hand for what's behind one of the doors. You get to choose which door. Come on, you came to make a deal, and now's your chance.

How many of us are going to trade what's in our hand for a chance on the wonderful things behind one of those doors? No one's going to give up God's love for a chance at material things, are we? Kinda sounds like your Sunday school teacher trying to fill your conscience with guilt, doesn't it?

But what if it was reversed one-hundred-eighty degrees? That is, you came with all the great material things in your possession (car, house, and money—lots of it) and Mr. Hall asked you if you wanted to trade that for what was behind the big curtain. This time you were told what's behind the curtain—it's God's love. Are you willing to trade what you

can i get there from here?

now have for God's love? Aren't we thankful it doesn't come to that?! But, how many of us have been tempted one way or another with thoughts like these? By the way, these past few paragraphs are no reflection on the TV show, *Let's Make A Deal*. And they're certainly no reflection on Monty Hall. They were just added to try to make a small point about life. I actually loved that show.

That should keep some of the potential lawsuits at bay...

Let's keep going.

are we all
god's children?

Hey, what's the deal?! I thought you said these would be simple yes or no questions, and now you go and try to get this stuff by us. Okay, calm down, let's start with the beginning—Adam and Eve. As stated earlier, this is *not* a book on religion or a history book on God and Jesus Christ. So why bring up the Book of Genesis? Well, probably because I don't know where else to start.

How about evolution, which was first discussed around nine hundred BC. Yeah, even back then it was a hot topic debated by scholars and theologians alike. The Old Testament is a historical book of books that has withstood the test of time (didn't I use that term somewhere else? Sorry!). It has withstood different religious beliefs (Jews, Islamics, and Christians to name a few), and withstood historical autopsies as to its authenticity. And each time, scholars, historians, and scientists agree that the books in the Bible are of historical value and can't be discounted with regards to their contribution to the history of our earth.

Add that to the fact that we still can't fully understand and explain how human life becomes life. By the way, this isn't a sex-ed book either, but we have to at least look at this. How does one explain a single cell, one single strand of DNA, coming together with another to multiply and divide? Then some nine months later, coming out a beautiful baby? (Why are all babies beautiful? Just a thought...)

So, the only conclusion I can come up with is that somewhere along the line, we all came from God. Yes, I know, I'm not an expert, and some of you are going to research the previous paragraphs to see how accurate I was. That's okay, this is my book, and since you already bought it, why not just go with the flow (so to speak). Why not just admit that at one time or another, we all have either heard the phrase, or spoken it, "He/She is a child/gift of God." Or something similar that I can't think of right now (Writer's block? Who knows, I never wrote a book before). But if you truly believe it, and have said it or heard it, then accept it. We're all children of God—even those who proclaim they're not!

And what if we look at Genesis? There's this guy Adam, and this gal Eve. They're ordered by God (remember, we already agreed that God exists) to populate the world. So, if we believe in God, then we have to accept not only that he loves us (previous chapter), but that what was written about him is true. So, both figuratively and literally, we're all children of God.

What about him being a loving God? Think about this:

Is it easier to love something when it's *yours*? For example, you see your neighbor pull up to his house in a new car; you yell across the street, "Hey, nice car!"

He replies, "Thanks, I just bought it."

"Do you like it?"

"Like it, I *love* it!"

Now we can say: "Oh, I love *your* dress," or "I love the way you decorated *your* house," or even "God, I love *your* car." But when we use the word love in that context, what are we trying to communicate? That we *really* like it; that we would love one, too? Probably something in that ballpark, don't you agree? But what about when it's *our* dress, *our* decorating ideas, and *our* car? We feel a different attraction about our stuff, even though we use the same word to describe it—*love*. Aren't we more devoted to something when it's ours than something that's *hers* or *his*? I use the word devoted because it's a synonym for love (at least in Microsoft Word). We can still feel a very strong affection to something (another synonym), without being devoted to it.

What about that chair that's upstairs in your bedroom? You know, the one that is *sooo* comfortable and sits by the window so you get the afternoon sun. The chair you plop into after a long day at work trying to get your students to behave, while at the same time being observed by the principal for your annual review. And what if you had a kid like me in your class? Boy, that chair feels great doesn't it? Especially with a nice hot cup of coffee after kicking off your shoes. Not a care in the world now!

Let me ask you, do you love that chair? You *love* the way it feels, the way it just absorbs your tired, weary body. You *love* the memories it holds, and the security it offers. That love equates to devotion, doesn't it? What would you do if when you got home after a bad day at work you discovered that the cat (there's that damn cat again) urinated on it? It's ruined now, isn't it? That feeling you now have is because you felt a sense of devotion, a sense of familiarity that only you can know when describing that chair. You've lost a sense of comfort, aware-ness, and security, as well as the memories. You really did love that chair—in the purest sense of the word.

Now, what if it was your neighbor's chair? Besides feeling bad and probably embarrassed that your cat ruined it, do you have the same feeling of loss that you had with *your* chair? Can you imagine being devoted to someone else's comfort-able chair? Even if you loved that chair, it didn't hold the same—*Je ne sais pas* (for my French teachers)—did it? It couldn't have, it wasn't yours!

What does *Je ne sais pas* mean? I don't know (you French students, give yourself 10 points there for that one).

That got me thinking. I know … I'm as scared as you are by now when that happens. But just give me a minute. I took three years of French in high school, passed two of them. Remember where I started as a paramedic? That city was predominately made-up of minorities with a strong Hispanic influence. Three years of French down the drain! But at least my seasoned partner in the ambulance taught me some of the "really good" Spanish words. So as not to think what they taught me was in vain, *Madame Kyler et Monsieur Skahan, merci beaucoup!* And when you're asked, "*Quel livre est-ce que tu veux?*" I hope you think, *Quel livre intéressant!*

Back to this book. So here's how I know we're God's children. It's his love! God couldn't love us the way that he does unless we are his. It really is that simple. You couldn't *really* love that other chair the way you loved your own chair, could you? Now take that feeling of love and imagine it in God's hands. We've already established that he is a loving God; so his love for us has to be out of this world (literally). That kind of love, that kind of devotion (as he's demonstrated countless times to each and every one of us) could only *come* from a parent. And that parent is our God. Looking at it another way: That kind of love, that kind of devotion could only be *given* to someone who belongs to the giver. And don't we all belong to God?

For those of you who bought this book, what do you say we go to the next question. By the way, if you bought this book—thank you! My kids now have a chance to go to college ... For those of you who "borrowed" it, or if you're the one who picks it off the shelf in Barnes and Noble, orders a cappuccino and sits down on a couch and reads it. Please, buy your own copy—remember my kids?

does he know us?

By that I mean does he know each and every one of us? Can we go to the New Testament for a minute? I promise, it'll be brief. If I remember right, I read somewhere that God knows each and every inch of us, right down to counting each strand of hair on our heads. Speaking of that, somehow my hair thinks it's a bird: it's migrating south, down my back. I guess you could say I'm living proof that God has a sense of humor!

Where were we? Oh yeah, the New Testament. Check out Matthew (Chapter ten, verse twenty-nine if you really want to be specific). "...*And even the very hairs of your head are all numbered.*" And now something from the Old Testament; how about Psalm 139: "*O Lord, you have searched me and you know me. You know when I sit and when I rise; you perceive my thoughts from afar.*" I only mention these two passages because they were written thousands of years ago. One attributed to the Son of God, and the other to a psalmist who never knew, nor could have known, Jesus. They believed—*or knew*—that God knew them way back then. So how does that affect me, in the here and now? Beats me, I was just searching for something to answer this question. No, not really. But I added the passages here to make a point.

Hold on a minute, I gotta go to the bathroom; I'll be right back.

Okay I'm back, I can think now. That's uncomfortable, don't you think; sitting there when you have to go, but you want to finish something? I mean, it's hard to concentrate when you gotta go. Now that I got that out of my system (add another ten points if you got that), let's see where we were. Does he know us? That was it, wasn't it? Okay, we agree he exists, we agree we are his children, and we agree he loves us. Why wouldn't he know us? I know, you can't answer a question with a question (thank you to Mrs. Merk, my fifth grade teacher for that). Let's make this simple, as in the first S in the KISS Principle.

If we're all God's children then he must be our father. Now think of the best father figure you know—maybe it's your own dad (mine's already taken) or someone you saw growing up or one portrayed in the movies. Whoever he is, think of all of his great attributes. Now imagine those attributes, those qualities, and that love in something as magnificent as God. Wow! We know his power, and we agree he loves us. Think of the awesomeness (I think that's a word, but I'm not sure) of his knowledge combined with the love he has for us. Someone that vast, someone that hears each and every one of us, has to know us. He made us.

Still not convinced? Try this: can you think of an inventor who doesn't know every part of his machine? Me either. The inventor took hours and hours of time and effort to know and understand each and every part; to know how they worked, and to know how they would work with each other, before he put the thing together. He probably studied some kind of engineering course (those know-it-all's really irritate me), and had years and years of experience before he got it right. Well, God has been "*building*" us for thousands of years. Do you think he knows what he's doing?

Let's put it another way: How well do you know your own kids? **If you are a kid reading this, whatever you do, don't become a parent now to try to understand what I'm saying—you're going to give your own parents a heart attack.** Sorry, I had to get that in there; I've got two teenage boys of my own...

We think we know them, don't we. Especially when they're young—like "little children age." It's when they are little children that we can really understand and know them because they haven't had their minds corrupted by the influence of the world around them. They haven't been exposed to hatred and ridiculed, they haven't seen the nastiness and cynical side of others. And if we, as parents, ever thought our children might come in contact with something that would hurt them (physically/emotionally/spiritually), we would scoop them up and protect them from it—even through the "terrible twos"! It's not until they have outside influences that we begin to lose that bond; they want to venture further and further away from the nest, and we're constantly trying to reel them back in. Are we more afraid of losing them or of them losing us?

God, I hate it when this happens. What was the point

can i get there from here?

I was trying to make? Can you imagine having me in your class in high school? At least you're getting a little glimpse of what my poor teachers went through—I never could sit still or stay focused for a very long time. How easily do you think I get bored? Oh crap, there I go again. Okay, stay focused (especially if I'm ever going to finish this book, at the rate I'm going this is going to take years), this is important.

God is our father and we are his children. We still agree on this, right? Can you find anywhere in the Bible, in scripture, in literature, where it says God intended for us to be his *adults*? How about being his *adolescents*, or *teenagers*? Nope, I couldn't find anything on that either, and this time I searched both Google *and* Yahoo. Can you imagine if we were his adults, adolescents, or teenagers? He'd want to kill us—no, not literally, but how many times have we said that about our own adolescents, teenagers, or adult friends? "I could just kill him/her for … (insert your own story/experience here)." They can make us crazy, can't they? How crazy do you think we make him?

He likes us the way we are; he loves us as his children. We are *God's children*, period, end of sentence. That's the way it's supposed to be. It's the way he intended it. That way, he will know us in a similar way that we knew our own children. I say similar because the power, knowledge and love we have for our children can't compare to his power, knowledge, and love for us. I don't think God's power, knowledge, and love can be quantified; but his attributes can be appreciated! So no matter how smart we think we are, how grown-up we think we are, how much experience we think we have, how much knowledge and understanding of the meaning of life we are confident we possess; yes, we are still the *children* of God! And as his children, he knows each and every one of us—by name!

What if we were to look at this another way? Have you ever been to a sporting event at a large stadium or arena? How many fans were in attendance? If it was a hockey or basketball game, probably no more than twenty thousand; if it was a baseball game, probably no more than fifty thousand. And if it was a football game; what do you think, about fifty or sixty thousand? Unless it's a college game, and then you're talking over one hundred thousand seats! Now that's a stadium.

Let's stick with a pro football stadium; maybe around sixty thousand seats. If you've ever been to one of these games, you know the excitement that's in the air. And it can get crazy. I get to go to these games whenever the home team is playing (I can't use the name of the team because of NFL rules regarding my employment). I say I get to go to these games because I'm actually working them. Is that too cool, or what? Sunday afternoons, as well as some Monday nights, I go to the stadium and work security at the games. Which basically means I'm one of the guys breaking-up the fights and throwing people out of the game—I mean politely escorting them to the nearest exit. Sorry, sometimes I get a little confused.

When you see a stadium filled to capacity, sixty thousand screaming fans, you get to thinking about how badly you're outnumbered! But what I also see is a stadium filled with God's children. Yes, I occasionally get a moment to reflect at these games. Sixty thousand people and God knows each and every one of them. And that's just one stadium. How many games are being played each Sunday? That number alone starts to put things in perspective.

can i get there from here?

I try to meet as many fans in my section as possible, and some of them I know by name; which gets me thinking. I can maybe remember a dozen or so names of the people in my section, and that's by the end of the season. Can you imagine knowing *everything* about these people I got to know? By that I mean to know so much about them you even know the numbers of hairs on their heads? That's just a handful of people. Now try to imagine standing at the entrance and memorizing the names of *every* fan that came to the game. Even if you're a genius, how many names—just names— do you think you could memorize? Forget about what they looked like, who their friends were, and what they liked to do; just try to remember their names.

If you gave me a list of names in alphabetical order, I don't think I'd get past the A's . Let's take this a step further. Somehow you were able to memorize the names, but just the first names. Did you think you were gonna have to remember their first *and* last names? Come on, let's not make this too difficult! So you got all of the first names of the people that are in the stadium. Now, memorize where they're sitting. Yep, what seat is John Smith in (sorry if that's your name—you are always getting picked on)? Give me his section, row, and seat number. One would be easy to remember, especially if that's all we had to remember. But we've been given the task of remembering everyone's seat location. Sound impossible? Okay, what if we just concentrate on our section? Maybe a couple of hundred people. Compared to the entire stadium of sixty thousand, a couple of hundred seems like a breeze. Imagine, if you can, standing at the bottom row of your section looking up at everyone's face. Now, start to identify each person by name, row, and seat number.

"You gotta be kiddin me!" I hear you. It's a daunting task, isn't it? Especially if you walked away and tried to write it all down from memory. Since I'm an overachiever, let's go another step. You're the lucky winner of a trip in the Goodyear blimp. You're now hovering over the stadium watching the game from a thousand feet in the air. Don't worry if you're afraid of heights or are thinking, "there's no way I'm getting into one of those things!" It's only a book, and we're using our imagination—it'll be okay, I promise.

So we're over this stadium filled with sixty-thousand-plus fans. Let's see if we can identify each and every one in the stadium. Not only identify these folks; but know their names, looks, birth marks, hair color/style, number of hairs, home address, occupation, birthday, business address, loved-ones' names, and whatever else you can think of. Could we even remember that much information about *one* person? Could we pick each person, by name, out of that crowded stadium? Remember, that's just one stadium in the country that particular Sunday. Just the task of knowing each of us seems like an unbelievable endeavor. And yet, he does it.

And not only that, he hears each and every one of us in that stadium. Not like a loud roar of the crowd on a touch-down run, more like we were sitting in a quiet coffee shop talking about old times. Imagine that, out of sixty thousand people talking to him in that stadium he is able to not only hear us—but to listen to what we are saying. And more often than not, it's what we're *asking*. Like children needing attention from their parents, God is there for us, listening to our requests. And he's able to hear each and every one of us. Not just in one stadium on a Sunday afternoon—but in every home, in every city, in every state, and in every country on earth! We are his children, and it's unbelievable that he can know each of us on such a personal basis.

Speaking of children, here's a thought. Why is it that when infants finally reach the point when they sleep through the night, that's the time their teeth start to come in? Sleep deprivation should never be used as torture, right? Told you God has a sense of humor.

Okay, next question.

did jesus live?

Come on, is this all you got? Of course he did and my dad gave him his middle initial, "H." It wasn't until I was taking confirmation classes that I found out Jesus didn't really have a middle initial. I spent most of my childhood trying to figure out what the H stood for: Harry, Henry, Hal, Hans...? It drove me crazy. But at least I knew when my dad was *really* mad at me. I swear my parents should have been saints; it would take two more books to describe what my brother, Glenn, and I did as kids. If this one sells, I'll start on the next one right away.

Another tangent, sorry. Hey, wanna know something? I just called out sick from work to write this chapter. Please don't tell my boss, he can be really cranky. Loveable, but cranky (I put *loveable* in there in case he decides to actually spend a few bucks and buy this book). God, I wish I could keep my mouth shut. At least you know why I've been a patrolman for twenty-two years and never promoted! Okay, focus; get focused.

Where do you want to start? Historians have agreed with

theologians on this one. Yes, Jesus lived; He walked the earth a couple of thousand years ago. Don't believe me? Wanna make a bet? How can you prove he *didn't* live? There I go again, answering a question with a question. Sorry, Mrs. Merk.

I have to go to the Internet. I can't go to the library and find a reference there, I called out sick, remember? I'd get crucified by my boss (note the not so subtle reminder of the way we throw around that term when we want to make a point) if he saw me out and about using precious sick time.

According to www.allaboutjesuschrist.org:

It is interesting that when people seek historic and scientific proof of Jesus, they immediately discount the Bible as a reliable source. If we look at the Bible simply as a historic document, it should be among the most reliable on record compared with others. Historians routinely cite Herodotus as a key source of information. He wrote from 488 BC to 428 BC and the earliest copy of his work comes from 900 AD (1,300 years later). There are only eight known copies of his work. By contrast, the New Testament of the Bible (with all its information about Jesus) was written between 40 AD and 100 AD The earliest known copy is from 130 AD and there are 5,000 known copies in Greek, 10,000 in Latin and 9,300 in other languages. Still, to put to rest the notion that there is no historic and scientific proof of Jesus outside the Bible, we may look to Jewish historian Flavius Josephus and to Roman historian Carius Cornelius Tacitus—both well known and accepted.

Josephus, in the book Jewish Antiquities" wrote:

"At that time lived Jesus, a wise man, if he may be called a man; for he performed many wonderful works.

He was a teacher of such men as received the truth with pleasure. And when Pilate, at the instigation of the chief men among us, had condemned him to the cross, they who before had conceived an affection for him did not cease to adhere to him. For on the third day he appeared to them alive again, the divine prophets having foretold these and many other wonderful things concerning him. And the sect of the Christians, so called from him, subsists at this time"
(Antiquities Book 18, Chapter 3, Section 1).

Tacitus, in writing about accusations that Nero burned the city of Rome and blamed it on Christians, said the following:
Nero procured others to be accused, and inflicted exquisite punishment upon those people, who were in abhorrence for their crimes, and were commonly known by the name of Christians. They had their denomination from Christus (Christ, dm.), who in the reign of Tibertius was put to death as a criminal by the procurator Pontius Pilate. At first they were only apprehended who confessed themselves of that sect; afterwards a vast multitude discovered by them, all of which were condemned, not so much for the crime of burning the city, as for their enmity to mankind...
(Tacitus, Annals, 15, 44).

Aren't you glad this isn't a book of facts, history, and other fun stuff all crammed together to try to prove a point? I'd have been asleep by now. By the way, is what I just copied and pasted plagiarism? I gave credit for the source of the information. I hope I didn't violate any copyright laws, I can't afford another lawsuit. Just kidding; no, not that I *can* afford a lawsuit, but that this would have been *another* lawsuit. Only once—and it wasn't my fault!

So as not to babble on, I underlined and italicized what I thought to be the *significant* parts of this significant article. I think they stand on their own merit and don't warrant any further discussion—I'm not here to insult anyone's intelligence. God knows, my own intelligence is subject to question. And speaking of intelligence, does anyone else not understand what "enmity" means (last line ... *as for their enmity to mankind*)? I had to look it up on dictionary.com. Still can't leave the house, not even to go get a sandwich.

Did you have to look up *enmity* too? Wouldn't *hate* or *hostility* be easier to understand in that sentence? What language do you think the Romans were using back then? Aren't you glad we learned how to speak English and not Roman? Yeah, I hear you, there's no such thing as The Roman Language. But there was an Ancient Roman Language; which, according to Wikipedia, has roots in the Latin alphabet—which is all Greek to me ...

For the sake of avoiding total confusion, let's see what another Roman historian, Suetonius, wrote around 112 AD:

"*Since the Jews constantly made disturbances at the instigation of Chrestus expelled them from Rome*".

Actually here's what he really wrote:

"*Judaeos, impulsore Chresto, assidue tumultuantes (Claudius) Roma expulit.*"

I wasn't sure who knew Latin, so I took the liberty of including the English translation. I had to look-up the word "Chrestus." It's Latin for the Greek name, Jesus.

From Greek to Latin (Ancient Roman?) to English. Any chances that we might have missed something in the translation? I think we actually could have. If you were to do a

Google or Yahoo search for Chrestus and/or the historian Suetonius, you would find two hundred fourteen thousand hits for Chrestus and two million three hundred eighty thousand hits for Suetonius. That's a lot of conversation about just these two characters! And the chances are different people have different interpretations about what Suetonius had to say about Chrestus. But the point is, at least three different noted and respected historians (Josephus, Tacitus, Suetonius) documented the life—or at least portions of the life—of a man named Jesus.

Hey, I told you the Bible was a historical document, and that was before I got this far in writing this chapter. I'm still not as smart as Mrs. Merk was, she was a great teacher; she gave me my first D on a report card.

Even though I got a D (actually, multiple D's) from Mrs. Merk, I have made strides in my reasoning skills—but not my vokaboolery yusij. Maybe it's the cop in me, but I just noticed something in the previous passages that made me wonder about something. You need to know that the paragraph that follows this discussion was supposed to be where this paragraph is. But when I thought of what we're about to look at, I used the Enter key on my computer to push that paragraph down so I could insert this before it.

What's it like to read what I'm trying to write? I can only imagine what you're going through, but try to stay with me; I promise it'll all make sense.

Here's what just jumped out at me: Josephus was a Jewish historian. Why would a Jewish historian—a recognized and esteemed author—write about Jesus if he didn't exist? Wasn't this about the time that Christians and Jews started to become at odds with each other? If Jesus was a myth, certainly a noted Jewish historian would have debunked that myth not only for the accuracy of history but for the people he represented. Instead, Josephus refers to Jesus as "*ho christos*"—The Christ or The Messiah. More translation, I promise it'll be the last.

A Jewish historian documenting Jesus' life and death. Who'd have thunk it? I've interviewed hundreds of suspects who denied the truth to either benefit themselves or someone close to them. Never have I had a suspect fabricate a story which would not only harm him, but those close to him. Suspects fabricate stories to get themselves *out* of trouble, not *into* it. So it seems to reason that if a Jewish historian was going to fabricate a story, he would certainly do so to help himself or aid his people, not the other way around.

We have historical documents of the life of Jesus, we have a religious book that goes into much detail about Jesus' life; and most of that book was written well before Jesus was born. His life was prophesied by Moses and Isaiah to name but a couple of prominent men. As stated in the plagiarized, uh, borrowed text above, there are tens of thousands of copies of the New Testament in so many different languages. Does anyone think that these books could have stood the test of time (here I go again with that term) if there wasn't some grain of truth to them? Or is the story of Jesus the original urban legend that has endured for thousands of years? I'll stick with the former; wanna join me on that one?

How about encyclopedias? These books are supposed to be accurate. I know I used a lot of them when I did my book reports. I referenced them and learned about footnotes from them. They are the accepted source of information in just about all of our schools. Here's a quote from one of them:

> *"These independent accounts prove that in ancient times even the opponents of Christianity never doubted the historicity of Jesus, which was disputed for the first time and on inadequate grounds by several authors at the end of the 18th, during the 19th, and at the beginning of the 20th centuries."*
>
> (Encyclopedia Britannica 1974 15th edition)

Historians, scholars, and even encyclopedias don't argue the existence of Jesus. There's a lot of debate about *who* he was; but little debate is left about *if* he was. That'll be brought up in a few pages from here.

Has anyone seen the documentaries on the Discovery and History channels about Jesus? Scientists looked into his story, and you know what? They (the "it has to meet scientific proof" people) say that Jesus lived—and that he lived about two thousand years ago, just like it says in the Bible. So are you telling me that scientists, the guys who say we came from apes (remember Darwin and evolution?) are now saying there's proof that a guy named Jesus was born in a manger, to a couple named Joseph and Mary? Yep, isn't it cool when science, history, and Christianity come together?

By the way, ever wonder what a manger is? We all have images in our heads of this cute little wooden house, with a little baby tucked nicely in hay lying in an even cuter wooden crib with more hay all around him. Here's how Wikipedia defines "manger":

a trough or box of carved stone or wood construction used to

can i get there from here?

hold food *for* animals *(as in a* stable*). Mangers are mostly used in* livestock *raising. They are also used to feed* wild animals, *e.g., in* nature reserves. *The word comes from the French mangeure, from Latin manducare, meaning chew.*

How many of us would see to it that our newborn was placed in a trough used to hold food for livestock? Talk about your humble beginnings...

From that humble beginning to the cross—what a life he led, what hope he offered, and what a promise he delivered. See how I segued this to the next question about the cross? Pretty smart, don't you think? Yeah, well Mrs. Merk would be proud.

I'll be back in a little bit, I'm going to take a chance and go to the store to get something to eat—I'm starving! Go ahead, you might as well get something too, I don't know how long I'm gonna be.

did he die on
the cross?

Two slices of pepperoni pizza and a large coke, some lunch don't you think?

Now we dig a little further into the life of Jesus; actually we fast forward to the end of it. His story was written by men of higher intelligence and of greater faith than me. If you want to check out his life, his work, his promise, and his gift may I suggest Matthew, Mark, Luke and John? I'm not even going to try to compete with them; they knew him as none of us ever will. It's their story, their understanding, and their books; let's leave his words to them.

But we can discuss his death on the cross. It's documented both historically and biblically. Go back and read the text from allaboutjesuschrist.org.—documented history that Pilate crucified Jesus on the cross. We've agreed on the following so far, haven't we: There is a God, God loves us, we are God's children, God knows us, and Jesus lived? Any dissenters? Good. Well it just seems to reason that if we take the last answer, Jesus lived, then he also must have died. Logic, what a beautiful thing.

So we have this guy named Jesus who lived about two thousand years ago (give or take a couple of decades). He traveled the land teaching and preaching about *his* God (*his* Father) in direct conflict with the law of the land at that time. Some really powerful leaders got really scared of him and what his followers might do, so He was condemned. One of the leaders, Pontius Pilate, captured him, tried him as a criminal, and ordered him put to death—in those days criminals were hung on a cross for their crimes. So, if we continue to use logic and the KISS Principle, Jesus must have been crucified on the cross, as criminals would have been in those days.

Want more proof? Ever look at all those necklaces with the crucifix hanging down? How about when you go into a church, what's up at the front? And if the crucifix is not at the front, take at look at some of the stained-glass windows. There's even a really, really big statue of the crucifixion on some cliff overlooking the sea in South America (who knows which country I'm talking about? Give yourself ten bonus points if you knew the answer). There's no way in hell (go ahead, let out a sigh—no ten points though) all these symbols of his death could be wrong, could they? Here's the thing that gets me: which one is the way he really looked on the cross? By that I mean did he have ropes tied around his wrists and ankles? Was there a small slanted platform where his feet rested, or were the nails the only things holding him to the cross? Some of the depictions show him with the crown of thorns on his head, while others don't.

Suggestion: Instead of seeing him on the cross with your eyes, try seeing him on the cross with your heart. Go ahead, try it now. Close your eyes and see him—really see him—with your heart.

Feels great doesn't it?

Finally, and we still have to agree that the Bible is a book of historical documents, check out the Old Testament. His death was foreseen hundreds of years before he died. Here ya go:

> *"And I will pour out on the house of David and the inhabitants of Jerusalem a spirit of grace and supplication. They will look on me, the one they have pierced, and they will mourn for him as one mourns for an only child, and grieve bitterly for him as one grieves for a firstborn son."*
>
> Zechariah 12:10 (NIV)

and

> *"Dogs have surrounded me; a band of evil men has encircled me, they have pierced my hands and my feet."*
>
> Psalms 22:16 (NIV)

Yeah, so that was just a couple of lucky guesses. You sure? Because hundreds of years later, here's what is written about it in the New Testament:

> *"When they had crucified him, they divided up his clothes by casting lots."*
>
> Matthew 27:35 (NIV)

Look at my hands and my feet. It is I myself! Touch me

and see; a ghost does not have flesh and bones, as you see I have."

Luke 24:39 (NIV)

"Here they crucified him, and with him two others—one on each side and Jesus in the middle."

John 19:18 (NIV)

Instead, one of the soldiers pierced Jesus' side with a spear, bringing a sudden flow of blood and water. The man who saw it has given testimony, and his testimony is true. He knows that he tells the truth, and he testifies so that you also may believe. These things happened so that the scripture would be fulfilled: Not one of his bones will be broken," and, as another scripture says, 'They will look on the one they have pierced.'"

John 19:34–37 (NIV)

After he said this, he showed them his hands and side. The disciples were overjoyed when they saw the Lord. Again Jesus said, "Peace be with you! As the Father has sent me, I am sending you." And with that he breathed on them and said, "Receive the Holy Spirit. If you forgive anyone his sins, they are forgiven; if you do not forgive them, they are not forgiven." Now Thomas (called Didymus), one of the Twelve, was not with the disciples when Jesus came. So the other disciples told him, "We have seen the Lord!" But he said to them, "Unless I see the nail marks in his hands and put my finger where the nails were, and put my hand into his side, I will not believe it." A week later his disciples were in the house again, and Thomas was with them. Though the doors were locked, Jesus came and stood among them and said, "Peace be with you!"

Then he said to Thomas, "Put your finger here; see my hands. Reach out your hand and put it into my side. Stop doubting and believe." Thomas said to him, "My Lord and my God!"

John 20:20–28 (NIV)

Look, he is coming with the clouds, and every eye will see him, even those who pierced him; and all the peoples of the earth will mourn because of him. So shall it be! Amen."

Revelation 1:7 (NIV)

Question: how could this historical event be foretold, and then when it occurred so many years later, witnesses write about it in the same manner?

The only conclusion I have is that *it* happened. Again, as with the creation of our earth, too many coincidences for it not to be the truth. By the way, ever wonder where we got the term, "Doubting Thomas?" Now ya know.

Look, I gotta share something with you. I don't want you to get the thought, especially at this point in the book, that I'm smart or have some kind of above average intelligence. Here's some proof by way of more disclosure about my past: I did not graduate in the top fifty percent of my high school class. I graduated in that percent which made the top fifty percent possible. To be more specific, I was proud to graduate in the top seven-eighths of my class.

Can you imagine in what percent of his class Jesus graduated? He was number one, numero uno, Valedictorian.

And he graduated number one in his class because he died on the cross—for each and every one of us.

Next question.

(This page intentionally left blank)

I always wondered why some of the text books I read had: "this page intentionally left blank" in them. Whether they were medical text books or legal criminal code manuals, I never understood why certain pages were intentionally left blank. It just never made sense to me. But it made them sound *really* important.

So I added a page, intentionally left blank, to make this book sound really important. If anyone knows the reason(s) behind the purpose of another one of life's mysteries (at least in my head) please e-mail me the rationale behind the idea of a blank page in a book.

did he know he was going to die that way?

Yeah, he knew. How do I know he knew? Well how you do know that I don't know that he knew? This could get really confusing. The damn cat's back on the keyboard, hold on a minute.

My shoe lace is now tied around a chair on the other side of the room, but at least I can get some work done. Boy, I'll tell you what; writing a book is a lot of work! Especially with all these distractions. You try typing with one shoe off and one shoe on—it's friggin distracting, I'm telling ya. Okay, let's get started here. But first, you should see Bojangles batting my shoe lace; he's on his hind legs swatting it like an amateur boxer. Hold on, let me take my shoes off, this is driving me nuts.

Admit it, if I were in your class, you'd have me tied to a

pole by now, wouldn't ya? There was no such thing as A.D.D. or A.D.H.D. back then. And there were *no* medications for a kid like me. Actually, there was one medication that worked— a phone call home from the principal. My prescription was my dad's belt. Hey, no such thing as child abuse back then either. It was called *discipline*, and you know what? None of us are any worse for the wear. Here I go with a sermon, I'm sorry! This time I really mean it, I'm going to stay on task.

Take a look at the Old and New Testament; I did. Jesus' life, and subsequent death, is prophesied. Jesus told his disciples that he was going to be put to death. He even knew which one was going to betray him, and who was going to deny knowing him. Yet, on that night, he sat with his disciples, his friends by that point, and ate dinner with them. He didn't wine and complain (add ten points if you got the intentional misspelling of *whine* and its correlation to the last supper). In fact, Jesus never complained about his living conditions or the condition he was about to be put in. All he did was heal people, teach others and serve God. The greatest man to ever walk on this planet, and he started out in a manger. No wonder people worship him!

How about distractions, since I brought them up a little bit ago. Can you imagine knowing when you are going to die? Can anyone imagine going through life with the knowledge of the suffering, humiliation, and execution that was to be his? Do you think that little tidbit of information might just be a distraction to us? You're damn straight! I can't think of what it would be like to know that on a certain date, at a certain time, I was going to be put to death—more appropriately, tortured to death. And knowing that if he really wanted to, my own father could stop it. And if my Father wasn't going to stop it, I would certainly run away, wouldn't you? Wouldn't anyone? I don't know what your definition of courage is, but I can't think of a more perfect example of it than Jesus' last days here with us. Yeah, Jesus faced a lot of distractions in his short time here, but he never complained.

Mrs. Merk never complained about me being a distraction in her class either; she just gave me a D and sent me to the office. Here comes the belt, ouch!

So Jesus lived knowing he was going to be put to death. He served his father knowing he was going to be betrayed, humiliated, condemned, tortured, and crucified. He didn't run, he didn't hide, and he never denied his purpose. He was the epitome of "The Loyal Soldier." Why would he continue to do what he did if he knew it would eventually lead him to his death? How many of us have that kind of conviction?

I just opened an e-mail that was actually safe to open at work. I usually don't get too many of them … I'm only a few years away from my pension, so I am careful about what gets opened and what gets saved for later. Actually, I guess I'm not doing myself any favors here because I just disclosed that I open personal e-mails at work. Any doubt now why I haven't been promoted? Okay, back on track: I got this e-mail and I think it would fit in good here.

Most of us would agree that Jesus, if he was just a man, could have stopped what he was doing and get with the program to avoid his death. But he had a plan; he was driven by a goal—to be our savior. And to that end, he gave himself to each and every one of us.

can i get there from here?

Some would say he went the extra mile, went one more degree further than any of us would.

What difference does one more step, one more mile make? We've all thought that, haven't we?

"If I hurry, I can get this done and it'll be okay."

"I know I could have spent a little more time on it, but it's good enough to get by."

"It's not gonna make that much of a difference, so this will have to do."

"I think I'll stop here, no one's gonna notice if I do anymore work on this."

Now imagine if Jesus had our thoughts? What if he actually said any of the above listed lines that so often come out of our mouths? What if he decided he didn't want to endure what he endured?

Do you think he ever thought, "Yeah right, Dad, that might be what you want, but it's easier to do it this way." How about, "I'm too tired to talk to all these people today, I'm going to quit at noon and take a nap?" We could have, "I could turn this water into enough wine for everybody, but I only have the time to make 20 glasses of it." Where would we all be today?

Instead, Jesus went the extra mile, took the extra step, and went one degree further than any of us could. What difference does one degree make? According to the e-mail I just opened from Nightingale-Conant, one degree can make *A lot* of difference. It's a link to a three-minute motivational movie. Here's the gist of it: Take hot water. When water is two hundred eleven degrees, it's hot. But at two hundred twelve degrees, it's boiling. And that one degree is the difference between a hot cup of coffee and boiling water. And boiling water creates steam. Think about it. At two hundred eleven degrees liquid is a hot (very hot) beverage; but at two hundred twelve degrees it can power a locomotive!

In other words, the difference between sitting down on that comfy chair sipping your favorite hot beverage and a steam boiler driving a train or ship is *one degree*. If that liquid didn't take the extra step or go the extra mile to rise from hot to boiling, there would be no steam. I never looked at it that way. Sometimes we're content with just doing the minimum to get by. It's said that Thomas Edison tried more than one hundred times to get his light bulb to work. What would have happened if he didn't take that extra step, go that extra mile—to make another degree of effort? I'm in the dark on that question...

So that's the difference one degree of effort can make. Can you think of anything that one degree more could make in your life? I know my life is filled with those thoughts. What if I only... What if I just... How come I didn't...?

Think about these facts from the video: Over the last twenty-five years, the winner of all the major golf championships won by an average of less than three strokes, for the past ten years, the winner of the Indy 500 won by an average of 1.54 seconds, and in the 2004 Summer Olympics, the winner of the men's 800 meter race won by less than three-quarters of a second.

The difference between winning and losing can be quite small. It's been proven in the three examples from the world of sports. But what about in life? We all know of those individuals who take it one step further and succeed. So what are we waiting for? I can't tell you—but you can probably guess—how many times I wished I did something, or had the guts to do something that I admired in someone else. Instead of com-

can i get there from here?

paring ourselves to others and their accomplishments, what do you say we both decide, right now, to stop procrastinating and take the bull by the horns (as my dad would say).

One extra step; just a little more time spent on these projects—our kids, our relationships, our hobbies, or even our faith—can make a huge difference. And that's the difference between sipping a hot cup of tea, and making a head full of steam. It's like our God taking that extra step, our Lord pushing it just one more degree, to ensure our salvation.

Jesus knew what was needed to ensure our salvation. Three gospels document what Jesus knew of his upcoming crucifixion:

> Now as Jesus was going up to Jerusalem, he took the twelve disciples aside and said to them, "We are going up to Jerusalem, and the Son of Man will be betrayed to the chief priests and the teachers of the law. They will condemn him to death and will turn him over to the Gentiles to be mocked and flogged and crucified. On the third day he will be raised to life!"
>
> *Matthew 20:17–19 (NIV)*

> They were on their way up to Jerusalem, with Jesus leading the way, and the disciples were astonished, while those who followed were afraid. Again he took the Twelve aside and told them what was going to happen to him. "We are going up to Jerusalem," he said, "and the Son of Man will be betrayed to the chief priests and teachers of the law. They will condemn him to death and will hand him over to the Gentiles, who will mock him and spit on him, flog him and kill him. Three days later he will rise."
>
> *Mark 10:32–34 (NIV)*

Jesus took the Twelve aside and told them, "We are going up to Jerusalem, and everything that is written by the prophets about the Son of Man will be fulfilled. He will be handed over to the Gentiles. They will mock him, insult him, spit on him, flog him and kill him. On the third day he will rise again." The disciples did not understand any of this. Its meaning was hidden from them, and they did not know what he was talking about.

Luke 18:31–34 (NIV)

So, to get back to the question—did Jesus know he was going to be crucified. Yep, he did. Remember, Jesus knew he was pissing off a lot of powerful people by his teachings and sermons. He also knew he was going to be tried and found guilty as a criminal. Knowing that, one has to come to the conclusion that he knew what his fate would be. Criminals were hung on the cross. So the answer to this question has to be a resounding *yes;* Jesus knew he was going to be put to death by crucifixion.

That takes care of the easy yes or no questions. And just in time, my feet are freezing. I gotta go put some socks on, I'll be right back.

can i get there from here?

they were the
easy questions?

Okay, I'm back and ready for round two. Can we take a minute and go over what we've covered so far? I do this methodical breaking-down of things as a way to solve problems. I've been solving problems like this for a while now and it seems to work well for me.

Wait, is it … it seems to work *well* for me, or … it seems to work *good* for me? I always get them confused. Mr. Parker's gonna be really disappointed; he was my high school English teacher and I know we went over this!

Okay, let's see: I'm *good* at this, or I'm *well* at this … I can think *good*, or I can think well … the steak is *well* done, or the steak is *good* done … did I do this *well*, or did I do this *good*?

Well, as my mom used to say: "Rusty, you know *good* and

can i get there from here?

well what I meant!" *Good*, now I got it. Don't you just love the rules of English?

Here's a question: Why do we drive on a parkway but park in a driveway? I could go on all day, but I've got to get this book done (is it *done* or *finished*?).

Moving on. If we used logic in the first part of this book, this is what we discovered:

- There is a God
- God loves us
- We are God's children
- God knows each and every one of us
- Jesus lived
- Jesus died on the cross
- Jesus knew he was going to be crucified

So in this order we know: God loves us as his children, and as his children, he knows us. Jesus walked on this earth a couple thousand years ago, and he died on the cross knowing the entire time he was going to be crucified for what he believed in.

Take a minute for yourself and see if you can't come up with a few more basic questions that might help you with some of the doubt(s) you're having. I think it's important to reflect back on this foundation and look at it from a perspective of how it impacts us. And remember, God expects us to have doubts. He knows there is no way we can understand his plan for us. No matter what you've thought of him, said to him, or acted against him—it's okay! Be gentle on yourself; he's not going anywhere.

Anyone remember the story *Footprints in the Sand*? It's

one of my favorites and one that reminds us God is there, *especially* during the bad times.

Did you refill your coffee? Are you ready for the second half? By the way, if I've offended anyone with my language or off-color remarks, sorry. See if you can get a refund; if not, give this book to a friend. Either way, I had to be true to myself in writing this, and this is just the way I am. I promise, nothing was meant by anything I said.

Except the part about my boss, he really can be cranky!

So let's get a hold of ourselves, and move on. No, no, no! Not that "get a hold of ourselves"! You really are sick; take ten points away—right now.

Now that Mr. Sicko is through, can we continue? What I meant to say is let's gather everything up that we've discovered and take it to the next level. But first, here's a question that really bothers me: Why don't they make a "B" cell battery for my flashlight? You've got A, AA, AAA, C, and D. What happened to B? Did the nine volt take its place? And why nine volts? Couldn't it be ten volts or eight volts or some other even number that makes sense? Still, why no B cell battery? I wish I knew who to write to.

I just looked it up on Google, and I am allowed to end a sentence with a preposition—I'm glad I got that over *with*.

Why was it so important to prepare the foundation we just laid? Well, first of all it filled the first part of this book, didn't it? Think about it, if the first part of this book didn't exist, then there couldn't be a second part. In that case, this second part would really be the first part, but then there still wouldn't be a second part. The good news: you would've been able to buy this book at half-price. Think about it!

Another tangent, I'm sorry. We had to lay the foundation, trusting in our beliefs. Or solidifying them—as in solid cement. Yeah, the stuff used to make foundations. The way I see it, if you're going to build something, in this case our faith, then you better have a good foundation to build it on. And once cement has dried and cured, it's solid, and for the most part, unmovable. That's why engineers insist on solid foundations before building something.

Would you agree that faith is a magnificent thing? A beautiful and majestic gift? Listen, even if you don't totally agree with this, I'm trying to make a point; so can you just say *yes*, you agree? Good, that makes it a lot easier. So we have this magnificent, beautiful and majestic building—our faith. Shouldn't it be built on a strong and solid foundation? Would anyone take a chance going to the thirtieth floor of a skyscraper knowing its foundation was made from sticks and rubble? Even if the inside of this building was featured in all the interior decorating magazines, even if photographs of it were featured in *Architecture Today* (just a guess at a trade magazine name), would you go up to the thirtieth floor knowing the foundation could crumble beneath you at any moment? Unless you're that guy from the first part of this book who would take a plane ride with a ten percent chance of making it, you're not even going to go inside this building let alone take the elevator to the top.

So we *cement* our faith knowing God loves us as his children, and as his children, he knows us. Jesus walked on this earth a couple thousand years ago, and he died on the cross knowing the entire time he was going to be crucified for what he believed in. There's no doubt about that now, is there? Did you know that synonyms for the word *cement* are: strengthen, bolster, reinforce, make stronger, prop up, and fortify?

Think about it, just by discussing and agreeing on a few basic points in the previous pages we have strengthened our faith, bolstered our faith, reinforced our faith, made our faith stronger, propped up our faith, and fortified our faith. What a foundation on which to build our...? How many words can we end this sentence with? A few that come to mind: relationships, beliefs, lives, and of course—our faith. Can you think of any more?

Now we can build anything we want on this rock-solid foundation of faith. So what do you want to build? Want to build a relationship with God? How about with his Son? Want to build a better understanding of his message? Want to build a knowledge of his teaching? What about a house? *Where did that come from?*

There are plenty of organizations looking for volunteers just like you and me to help them build a home for someone who needs one. And you don't need any special skills or tools; in fact you don't need to know anything about construction at all. I dare you, right now, to put this book down and go look up the number for one of those organizations in your area. You don't have to call right now, but how about if you put the name and number someplace where you'll know where they are later.

Why not think about the foundation you already built— all by yourself. Well, not really by yourself; ya had a little help along the way, didn't ya? Go ahead. I'll wait for you to express your gratitude to the one who has guided you through this journey so far.

No, not to me.

Are you out of your mind?! I wasn't the one who helped you; I wasn't the one who was with you as you read this, and I wasn't the one who will *always* be there *with* you, *for* you, and *within* you. No, I'll wait while you acknowledge and thank *him*.

Take your time; I gotta go to the bathroom again anyway. Before I go (get it, before I *go*—another ten points if you rolled your eyes) do you want to know another factoid about me? I was going through some stuff from the attic a couple of weeks ago and I came across my baby book. Guess what my very first sentence was? "I build a house."

What kind of house... How big... What shape... Where... How much will it cost... For Who (or is it For Whom—sorry Mr. Parker)... What materials should I use... What color should I paint it... How should I decorate it? Wow, sometimes I think God drops these little hints just to watch me go out of my mind! Do you ever feel like that? Do you ever ask yourself if there's a message in there somewhere? Well at least I know I have a solid foundation to build it on.

Be right back.

I'm back. That didn't take as long as I thought—TMI, huh? I pulled all that together and packaged it pretty neat, don't you think? Come on, you have to admit—foundation, cement, faith, build, and then bringing it back to foundation again.

Even I'm surprised at how I pulled that together. Can we please move on now (I can hear you ...).

To the open-ended questions. Let's start with an easy one, and then move forward to tougher ones. That's the way I tackle a problem, take out the easy part first and concentrate on the tougher ones. So here we go.

why was jesus sent to us, and whose idea was it?

To save us—from ourselves. Simple enough!

Okay, you dropped a couple of bucks for the book, so we should talk a little about it. Unless you're that guy who sat his rear end down at Border's and read this thing for free! I'm telling ya something, I got friends who owe me favors...

No, go ahead, read the rest of it now. I just feel bad for the next guy who sees it, buys it, and when he gets home, finds that you dog-eared the pages when you got up to go the bathroom. Question: Do those bookstores allow you to bring merchandise into the bathrooms? I once walked into the men's room at Home Depot with a plunger in my hand... and... uh... well, never mind.

Okay, just a little history lesson—it won't be long, I promise. Remember Adam and Eve? Yeah I know, I never really got to a point with that, did I? Sorry. Maybe it was meant to be that you would have to wait until now to see the point I was trying to make. Huh, ever think of that? More than likely, it was because of the cat. Remember, when in doubt, blame the cat. Okay, so here goes my history lesson (and it wasn't learned from Mrs. Merk—although back then you could actually say Merry Christmas in school!).

Adam and Eve—original sin; ring a bell with anyone? You see, our problem from the get-go was sin. No one is exempt from it and we're all going to keep committing sins until the day we die. It's just a fact of life. So what was God to do for our salvation and his heaven? Somewhere in time he chose the exact date that he would send his Son to us, to save us. By that I mean to die for *our* sins so that *our* sins would be forgiven. Basically, Jesus was going to take the heat for the rest of us. During the days of the Old Testament, the only way one could be forgiven for sin was to offer an animal sacrifice. But that only *covered* sin; it really didn't take it away.

When Jesus came to us, Jewish culture was in trouble. In addition to the Law of Moses, additional laws were being placed on the people. It was getting so bad that spiritually, people were questioning everything—especially who was actually leading them in the right direction. So I guess (I have to make an educated guess at this one) God knew it was the right time to try to right the ship, so to speak.

"Pasta with Vodka sauce, yeah that sounds good, hon! Can I have some garlic bread, too?" Sorry, I'm getting hungry; I haven't eaten anything since those two slices of pizza. Trust me; she's a goo-ood cook! I'll let you know when it's ready. Why don't you go start something now so we can sit down and eat together? I'll wait.

Speaking of hungry, do you think 2000 years ago people were hungry and thirsty? Do you think they shared a hunger for truth and a thirst for salvation? And isn't it written somewhere that God will give us what we need? It's obvious that the people of *that time* needed Jesus at *that time*. And everything he said and did happened for them and for everyone who has come and gone since. In other words, for all of us.

Jesus was sent here for us. The most quoted passage of the Bible tells us so; I'd be a fool not to state it here:

> For God so loved the world that he gave his one and only Son, that whoever believes in him shall not perish but have eternal life.
>
> John 3:16

What's that, twenty-six words long? Can you think of any other sentence that has the meaning and impact that this simple twenty-six-word sentence delivers? Me either! I think that just about covers this topic. Shall we move on?

We believe in Jesus—as stated earlier. And as far as I could find, there's no other story, no other documentation, no other theory than the one that's been on the table for the past twenty centuries. His father, God, sent Jesus to earth. Not just to earth, but to *us*. Think of Jesus as the ultimate Christmas gift (come on, too easy; don't give yourself anything for that one) given by the ultimate gift giver. God must have known the time was right to have his Son try to knock some sense into us. From what I've read, nothing else seemed to work for very long, so he probably had no choice. I mean think about it, what kind of father would send his only Son to people who were just going to kill him anyway? I'll tell you what kind of father: The One who is the ultimate gift giver; the Father whose love for his people cannot be measured; the Father who knew he had to do it.

That's why, when I find myself questioning God and his actions, I force myself to remember what he gave me. Yeah, he gave Jesus to me, personally. Tell me that's not the most awesomest (probably not an actual word) gift you could get? Can you believe it? God gave his Son to me! But he also gave Jesus to each and every one of you. How he did it, I don't know. Did you ever get something so spectacular that you wanted to just savor the moment? Well, that's what I'm doing. Jesus is here for each and every one of us; especially me.

In John 7:28–29 (NKJV), Jesus said, "I have not come of myself, but He who has sent Me is true, whom you do not know. I know him (God) and He sent Me."

That was easy.

why did jesus have to be born from a virgin?

Okay, can you imagine what it must have been like for Joseph and Mary? I mean, come on; were you ever afraid of dropping or spilling something in the kitchen or dining room? The event was so important (say Christmas or Thanksgiving), and everyone was watching as you tried to pull the turkey out of the oven, or tried to get the casserole to the table without dropping it. You remember the pressure, don't ya? Or what about being invited into a really expensive house, with really expensive things, and you decided to bring along your five-year-old? Talk about pressure! Now here's Mary (I almost added *and Joseph*) carrying what was the most precious cargo mankind would ever know. And Joseph—he was her escort—making

can i get there from here?

sure the cargo was handled properly and got to its destination safely. Nah, no pressure, right? Sure, we could do that.

Look, I can't even get my dog's water bowl from the sink to his crate without spilling it all over the floor. And watch out if I'm walking down the hall with a cup of coffee, Holy Mother of God (another attempted pun, add ten points if you think it was timely for this chapter). The more I concentrate on it, the more it spills. Have you ever tried to get in step with the movement of the coffee inside the mug? Almost impossible! How do waitresses do it?

Am I allowed to say waitress? I don't want to come across as sexist or politically incorrect. Let's see, we don't have stewardesses anymore, they've become flight attendants; they're no longer secretaries, they are administrative assistants; janitors are custodians, and what else did I forget? Oh yeah, the kid pumping my gas is a fuel delivery specialist and the garbage man is a refuse transfer expert. Cut me a break!

Another tangent, and the cat's not even around. Did I ever tell you about the time I was in Ms. Fredericks' Discussion and Debate class in high school? I took the affirmative on Euthanasia. Both teams decided on the topic I gave her the week before the debate. I gave it to her verbally; didn't write it down. Well, since I took the affirmative, I got to go first. Remember I said I gave the topic to Ms. Fredericks *verbally*. That's because I was debating for "Youth In Asia" (sounds identical, doesn't it?) How could the other side debate against the poor children in Asia? I never saw her that pissed-off. Well, not until the next time I had to present a topic. This time she was smart, she made me *write it down*. "Bussing;" can't make it much simpler than that. No misspelling there.

So here comes my turn to present after a week of preparation. They prepared for the controversial topic of putting children in school buses and sending them across town to another school, to achieve racial equality. Me, I presented for the issue of the teenagers who clear tables in restaurants. Bussing, one word with two meanings.

And another trip to the office...

"Hi Mr. Morgan, it's me again." "Yeah, I know, but come on, even you laughed when you saw the write-up!" "All right, I'll stop; but I don't think she likes me!" Mr. Morgan: my disciplinarian and the person who introduced me to the school disciplinary code starting my freshman year.

Okay, I'm back. Look, this isn't easy—coming up with things to say. You try it. You have these thoughts in your head, and you put them all together and they make perfect sense. Then you try to put them on paper, and your fingers can't keep up with your brain, so things get all screwed up. Then you try to remember what the hell you were thinking about in the first place and before you know it you're totally lost and confused. That's where I was. And I thought to be fair to you, the consumer, I would add some thoughts to what otherwise would have been a blank page in the book. No thoughts, no words—right? So for you, I rambled on about another proud moment in my childhood so you wouldn't be looking at a blank page or two. Now my thoughts are back, so we can move on.

Let's forget about the pressure of carrying the world's savior. Imagine the performance anxiety in conceiving him? There's no way that was going to happen. I can't even imagine how the conversation would go after dinner. Yeah I can: "Hey, Mary, you're not going to believe this dream I had..."

can i get there from here?

Nope, not going there! I can't, lightning hasn't struck me or this laptop yet, and I'm not going to take any chances. Sorry if I disappointed anyone. If you think you have a clever little one-liner on the subject, e-mail it to me. But can't you see what that would have opened up? Questions, accusations (like she didn't get any of those, right?), comments, and a lot of material for the late night comics.

Jesus was conceived from the Holy Spirit because he was perfect. And perfection can only come from God. God knew this, and he knew what the consequences would have been if it was done any other way. So God created his Son in Mary's womb. Jesus was perfect, and without sin. Mary was pure; Joseph had no marital relations with her, according to Matthew 1:25. And because she was pure Mary gave birth to our savior.

I gotta take a breath after that one.

why did jesus have to die the way he did?

Wow, that's a question that I'm gonna have to research a little bit. Let me check my handy Internet and I'll be right back. Go take a break or walk the dog, or take your dinner out of the oven. I hope it's not burnt. I'm going to eat mine while I look into this a little bit further. *Bon Appetite*.

Man, there's a lot of stuff out there on this topic. Remember, this is just my opinion obtained from other opinions on the subject. Scripture appears clear on this topic, but there are different opinions.

Hold on, I gotta wipe the butter from my garlic toast off the space bar.

All agree that Jesus had to suffer so that our sins could be forgiven. But why? Why couldn't he just be killed quickly and painlessly? Why did he have to suffer being whipped, having thorns pushed into his head, being spit on and mocked, and then being stabbed in the side? All to be hung on a cross and die. Once again, we find ourselves surrounded by so many questions.

Let's start with Isaiah, Chapter 53, verses 4–6 (NIV):

> *"Surely He took up our infirmities and carried our sorrows; yet we considered him stricken, smitten by him, and afflicted. But He was pierced for our transgressions, he was crushed for our iniquities; the punishment that brought us peace was upon him, and by His wounds we are healed. We all, like sheep have gone astray; each of us has turned his own way; and the LORD has laid on him the iniquity of us all."*

If I read this correctly, it means:

Jesus has taken our infirmities (sickness and pains)—probably the spiritual and emotional stuff:

By being pierced—he assumed our transgression (wrong doings);

By being crushed—Jesus assumed our iniquities;

By being punished—he gave us peace;

By his wounds—he made sure we were healed.

Isaiah concludes by comparing us to sheep that have gone astray. But we are spared because God has given Jesus all of our sins.

All the things that were done to him, he endured for us.

Yet for all that he took for us that day on the cross, he also gave to us. He gave to us his love—God's love. And that love was promised to all of us.

Here's what Paul had to say on the subject:

> *"Scarcely for a righteous man will one die; yet perhaps for a good man someone would even dare to die. But God demonstrates His own love toward us, in that while we were still sinners, Christ died for us"*
>
> Romans 5:7–8 (NKJV)

And he added this in Romans 6:23 (NKJV):

> *For the wages of sin is death, but the gift of God is eternal life in Christ Jesus our Lord.*

That's what I call love. God demonstrated his love for us. Even though we're all sinners, God allowed his *Only* Son to die for us. Simply because he loves us. Maybe we all need to be reminded of the pain and suffering Jesus went through for us. Maybe his pain and suffering are supposed to be an example of his love for us.

We live in a violent society. Hey, I'm a cop remember? You don't have to remind me of violence. You should know that I'm a cop assigned as a school resource officer in a high school. I've been there for eight years now, and I get to see first-hand the violent nature of our youth. The violent nature of *our future*. Can I tell you, it scares the hell out of me? Here's another opinion of mine: Our kids are becoming numb to the violence they see and experience. Not only are they becoming numb *to the* violence, they are becoming insatiable *with it*.

They want to see and partake in more and more of it. What was popular last year is out this year. Just look at the TV shows and the video games. The more violent they are, the more popular they are. Some ass-hole even produced a video game glamorizing the Columbine High School tragedy. As my mom would say, we're going to hell in a hand basket! Sorry if I offended anyone with the asshole comment, but it's the only word I could think of that accurately describes the scum who think of glorifying these things.

Wow, that was pretty heavy stuff, don't you think? Let me try to lighten it up a little bit. Remember my accounts of getting in trouble with Mrs. Merk and Ms. Fredericks? Well they were only two out of dozens of teachers and school faculty who I had the distinct pleasure of pissing off. I shouldn't say pleasure, because they were both really good teachers and they certainly didn't deserve a kid like me in their class. But here's my point...

Almost went off on another tangent there; you wouldn't believe what I was going to write! Whenever I would get in trouble, I got sent to the office. This pattern started in third grade. Being the over-achiever I was, I continued to increase my journeys to the office each year, right through my junior year in high school. I did have the pleasure of meeting principals, school board members, and school counselors during my tenure in each school. Each principal had his own set of rules and own ideas about punishment. It ranged from an apology to the teacher, to a detention, to a suspension. Hey, at least I never got expelled! It's not that I didn't try, though.

Anyway... I lost where I was going with this... School, office, detention, suspension—now I remember! Whether it was me or Keith or Ralph or Dave or John or Bill (I'll refrain from using last names here), the punishment was spelled out in the school's disciplinary code. The school disciplinarians would read the disciplinary report, look it up in the code, and then hand out your punishment.

God doesn't have a room for detention, does he? How can he suspend us for screwing up? He tried just about everything to show us how much he loves us. But we just keep on sinning, and partying and having a grand time; throwing his commandments and wishes out the window. What is he to do?

Imagine a school principal who loved his students so much, he wanted to give them a gift. He wanted to show the students that their behavior would be forgiven, in the way of a gift. But that gift had a *Huge* price tag. If he gave the students this gift, he knew that the majority of them would straighten-up and fly right. But it would cost him. His most beloved possession, his child, would be taken from him and killed. That would be the ransom for his students to start behaving. I have gotten to know a lot of principals (no, not that way, I mean as a school resource officer) over the past decade, and they are some of the most dedicated professionals I have ever met. But as dedicated and devoted as a principal is to his school and his students, I can't imagine him sacrificing his own children for his students. That doesn't make him a bad person, and it doesn't mean he doesn't care about his students. It just means that principals aren't God! And who would expect that from a principal, anyway?

I just burped up my dinner. I swallowed the burp! Oh, it burns... Vodka sauce *does not* taste better the second time around. Give me a minute; I gotta go take a couple Tums.

Okay, I'm back, but boy do I have a strange taste in my mouth. So we had this principal who didn't care enough about his kids to give up his only son for them. And the same principal who was going to have his son taken away from him so his students' behavior would be forgiven would have to watch his son be tortured and killed in front of him. In fact, he would be given a front row seat to the execution. As a father, I can't begin to imagine having to watch my child suffer. I can't stand it when either of my sons is in any kind of pain, let alone being tortured right in front of me. How about you, do you have any kids of your own? Maybe you have nieces or nephews, or younger cousins? Can you imagine sitting by helplessly while a child is taken from you, publicly humiliated and degraded, then tortured until he or she suffers an agonizing death? And what would you do when they screamed out for you to help them; when they cried out for you, asking why you turned your back on them? How barbaric do we have to get here? It's pretty heart wrenching, isn't it?

I would imagine, if you could ask him, Jesus would tell us he still can feel the stinging of the whips, the pain of the beating, and the tearing of his skin, muscles, tendons, and ligaments as the nails were driven into him. I don't think you forget that kind of pain. And what about the torment and humiliation he endured dragging his cross through the streets to the mount? What about the betrayal he felt from his friends and those who saw him go through the streets?

Would *any* of us ever forget *any* of that? I don't think Jesus does, either. Every day he's reminded of his own agony and suffering. And how is he reminded of that? Probably with *our* sins... And yet, there he is, up there with his Father, making sure we're okay down here. Making sure our sins don't send us to damnation and eternal pain and suffering. So how can I complain of heartburn and indigestion, demand that drug companies find a medicine that makes me feel better even faster, while Jesus was tortured for me? Am I a self-centered, egotistical spoiled brat, or what?

Why did Jesus have to die that way? He had to die, being tortured on the cross, so that we could have eternal life.

Sorry if that didn't lighten it up like I said I would try to do.

Does anyone have some Maalox?

what's the bible?

A book you don't see in Catholic churches! God, I crack myself up. I know they have one; it's up on the altar. That reminds me, A priest, a rabbi, and a nun walk into a bar (stop me if you've heard this)... Okay, I'll stop; but come on, don't take yourself (or your religion) too seriously. Can't we take time to laugh at ourselves? And speaking of laughing, let's see what the Bible says about laughter.

Would you believe I just read the entire Bible and counted each time there was a reference to laughter? You really are getting to know me, aren't you! I Googled it; I admit it. Hey, there are a lot of good websites out there in regards to the Bible; you oughta give it a try of you have the time. But remember what I said at the beginning of this book; take what you read with a grain of salt...

The Bible has forty-two; count 'em, forty-two references to laughter. And to show you just how much I really did look into this, here's a couple that I found in the New King James Version:

Psalm 59 (verse 8): *"But you, O LORD, shall laugh at them; you shall have all the nations in derision."*

Psalm 37 (verse 13): *"The Lord laughs at him; For He sees his day is coming."*

Proverbs 1 (verse 26): *"I also will laugh at your calamity."*

Okay, you say, they were referring to God laughing, but it doesn't seem in a very funny way. You're right; at first I thought I would list all forty-two, so I started with the first ones I could find. But then I changed my mind and decided to end with this, also found in the New King James Version:

> Luke, Chapter 6, Verse 21: *"Blessed are you who hunger now, For you shall be filled. Blessed are you who weep now, For you shall laugh."*

So here Luke tells the people that their sorrow (weeping) will turn into laughter. Why would he use the term laughter to counteract sorrow? It has to be good, that's why. And I'll end this tangent on this: Just before my dad died he made me promise him something.

"Promise me that you'll never take yourself too seriously."

"Sure, Dad."

He continued, "Because when it's all said and done the number of people that show up at your funeral is going to depend on one thing and one thing only."

"What's that, Dad?"

"The weather that day!"

Of all the things my dad taught me, that is the advice I

remember most. Betcha couldn't have figured that one out. So please, take my dad's advice. Come on down off that perch, humble yourself, and for God's sake—laugh. Laugh at yourself—you're the best material you could want if you become a comedian! Can we just agree that for the remainder of this book, neither one of us will take ourselves too seriously? Thanks, that would make my dad happy.

So where were we—that was a long tangent—Ah yes, the Bible. Well, we know for sure that it's a book that contains forty-two references to laughter. But what else is it? Let's review. There is a God, who knows each one of us and loves each one of us. He sent his Son to us so our sins would be forgiven. We also agree that the Bible has withstood the test of time, both historically and rationally.

It really isn't one book though, is it? Rather, it's a compilation of numerous books related to one topic. And that one topic—whether you're a Christian, Jew, Muslim—is about God. The same God who exists, who knows each and every one of us by name, who loves us, and who sent his Son to us. So, the Bible is about the One who wants us to read it. Well, maybe not read it from cover to cover, but how about understanding what he wanted from the beginning (remember Genesis?).

If we look at this rationally there is a God and the Bible is an accurate historical book (or book of books). Put them together and what do you have? How about an accurate historical book of God. A book that has accounts that were authored by different people from different backgrounds and at different times. Yet, they all point in the same direction, to the same thing. They point to a powerful and almighty God (Old Testament) who loved us so much (Old and New Testament) he sent his one and only Son to us (New Testament). How could so many prophecies—written by different people and at different times—be so true and become fulfilled by Jesus? Maybe, just maybe, the Bible is *that* accurate.

And if the Bible is that accurate—about God and Jesus—then I believe we must accept it as that which God wants us to know. Because, if you think about it, the Bible covers everything we really need to know—from the beginning (Genesis) to the end (Revelation); from birth (Christmas) to death (Easter).

One more thing. Did you know that there is an *estimated* 2.1 billion Christians in the world? How many clergy administer to these 2.1 billion people? I'm not gonna do the math, and I don't feel like searching Google, but how many people would be left jobless without the Bible (go ahead and give yourself ten extra points if you figure this out)? If there's no Bible, then we don't need anyone to interpret it and explain it, right? No Bible, no clergy; it's that simple.

And if there's no clergy, then we have no churches, and no churches means no religion; and no religion means no faith. Now, let's take it a step further (try to keep up with my brain). No Bible=no clergy=no churches=no religion=no faith. What about the workers? No religious holidays for those much-needed 3-day weekends or middle-of-the-week breaks, which translates into less shopping at the malls during those days off. No more parochial schools, so those teachers need to find other jobs which hurts the economy even further because who else but Catholic school students are going to buy those uniforms? And what about Easter? There goes the chocolate industry. Of course, we all know that Christmas is all about ____ ____ing, right? Can you imagine all those stores in the ____ ____ out of business because there were no more holid____ ____ Economic disaster all the way around. See, God ____ ____v what he needed to do to keep the economy goir____

Question: Ho____ ____h of the time that we're off for religious holidays d____ ____ really take the time to remember why we're off in t____ ____ place? Just another day to sleep-in; after all, we wo____ed hard and we deserve it! What about Easter? Yeah, it w____ ____ ____ the two days I went to church each year, too. But ____ ____e ham dinner and nice flowers, why else are we off on ____ood Friday (for those of us in the public sector)? How ____bo____ Christrmas, besides being *the other* day I went to chu____ch; re____mber that little baby, born of the virgin, lying in th____ ____ ____r are we too caught up in finding the perfect gift?

____ps the Bible just might be a reference book for us to ____ ____ to remind us of what those holidays are supposed to be ____ ____. Perhaps it brings together clergy, church religion, and f____ h, and gives meaning to this life by having us ask questions about its content. By the way, am I the only one who absolutely goes out of his head when I see: "Merry *X-Mass*?!"

So, by definition, as we discussed earlier, the Bible is an accurate historical record of the events of our world, from the very beginning! Are you like me and wish you could pick and choose which passages or books from the Bible are the ones you agree with? Take Genesis; come on, an entire world in seven days? You gotta be kiddin' me! The Ten Commandments; yeah they might have been pertinent back in *those* days, but times have changed. Are you telling me that stealing is just as bad as murder? You can steal as much as you want in this country and no one's going to put you to death for it. But kill someone in Texas, man they're gonna fry your butt. And what about what Jesus said? Too many rules for me; I think I'll just take the really important ones—you know, the ones that I can live with.

Or better yet, why not re-write it, you know: "*The Bible for the Modern Sinner.*" We can make an addendum to the New Testament, you know, at the end right after the book of Revelation. By the way, who wrote that and were they high on something? I've read it, reread it, and even tried to read it backwards (like playing the Beatles album backwards to see if Paul's dead); I still can't figure it out.

So that's it. We'll just re-write what we want to be in there, and take out whatever we don't want or don't agree with. After all, this is the twenty-first century, and we're entitled to a "New Amended Bible," aren't we? It's kind of like changing a grade on your report card before it gets home to mom and dad. You really did *earn* that "F," but you think you did better, and she was out to get you anyway. So what's the harm in bumping your grade up a few points?

That's what I did after Mrs. Merk gave me my first D. That was the second marking period and I had four more (marking periods) to go. So what do you think I did the third marking period? I became resourceful. After discussing the D with some of my trusted colleagues, it became apparent that I couldn't change a D to another grade without making it too obvious. Remember, this was before computers spit-out your report card and sent it directly home to your parents. Back then, teachers had to actually *write* the letter grade in a little box for each subject and for each marking period. If you were a little creative, and had a black pen, you could take care of business.

So, the third marking period rolled around and I had a choice: Change my troublesome ways and get with the program, or take the easy way out and just use my black pen at the end of the marking period. By now you know the answer. I was able, in six short weeks, to take my D to a solid F. I told you I was an over-achiever! Report card time came and I sat anxiously in my seat to be called up to Mrs. Merk's desk, as we all did back then, to be handed my report card *personally* by my teacher. Not for nothing (for my North Jersey readers) but having your name at the end of the alphabet really sucks when you're waiting for something like your report card. I got back to my desk, pulled it out of the envelope and opened it. There it was, like a shining star—my first F! What a proud moment in my educational history. Ah, but not to worry, *my friends and I* had a plan. On the way home from school, we stopped at the pavilion by the beach, took our gloves off (this was right before Christmas vacation—yes, you could actually call it that) and went to work. Very carefully I added the top curve to the *F* so it looked like a capital *P*. Now for the bottom arc; careful now, can't screw this up. Slowly and deliberately I ran my pen in an arc connecting the arc of the *P* to the bottom of the letter, forming a perfect capital letter *B*—my *new* grade.

My mom was so proud—I took a D and brought it up to a B. Wow! The next morning, she signed on the "parent signature" line and added this to the "parent comment" line: "We're so proud, keep up the good work!" I took my *signed* report card back to school and then it hit me. Holy Crap–I forgot the report card had to be returned to Mrs. Merk—

Signed! Hopefully she'll just check to see if it was signed and move on to the lessons for the day. Can anyone guess what kind of luck I had as a child and what kind of luck continues for me as an adult?

Yep, if it wasn't for bad luck… Mrs. Merk went through all the report cards, quickly glancing at them to make sure they were signed. Until she got to mine. Not only did she check to see if it was signed, she actually took the time to read my mom's comment. That comment, that one little "proud moment" comment caused Mrs. Merk to double-check my grades on the front. As soon as she looked up over her glasses I knew I was screwed. Another trip to the office; another phone call home, and this time my father offered me the opportunity of picking out the belt of my choice.

Ouch!

Why did I add that little story—another moment of my life that caused me pain? Because as I write this section on the Bible I get to thinking: do we take out of it (the Bible) only what we want to hear? If we think about our lives, have we ever changed an *F* to a *B*? Am I the only one who's ever rationalized my behavior/decision/actions to fit my needs? By that I mean don't we sometimes take the F's (our failures, poor decisions, bad decisions, etc.) and make them righteous by rationalizing them (changing them to B's) to ourselves and others? So what's the difference between that and changing an F to a B?

And even after we're called out on it, how many of us come up with excuses to cover our rationalization? A never-ending vicious cycle of denial, rationalization, excuses, poor decisions, denial…

We really are full of ourselves, aren't we?

The Bible is what it is and what it always has been. Not complicated, not wavering, and not edited for our satisfaction. Simply the truth—the way God wanted us to know it. We're still not rocket scientists, are we? By the way: Do you think God has a belt?

You bet your ass he does!

I don't think I ever answered one of your questions at the very beginning of this book. "What are my qualifications to write a book like this?" I don't have a precise answer. You know, one filled with degrees, education, and all that stuff. But my impressive resume does say the following: "high-school slacker, college dropout, divorced parent of two, struggling financially, living paycheck to paycheck, searching for answers, has questioned his faith, and has said some pretty embarrassing things to God."

Now that's an impressive resume! As you've seen so far, my life's been somewhat colorful, as my mom would say. I bet you can't wait to see what happens next. Are you reading this now for a discussion on faith or to see how much more trouble I got into as a kid? Just asking. How about moving on to the next question? But before we do, I have an ethical question regarding etiquette. As you know I'm writing this on a laptop (IBM ThinkPad to be exact), and by definition, a laptop computer is portable. I've stopped my writing a couple of times to go to the bathroom, but kinda lost my train of thought when I returned. Here's my question: Would it be improper to take this into the bathroom and continue writing while I ... uh ...

My parents would be so proud of me. I can hear my mom now: "Just look at our son; he's so clever, and he can really

can i get there from here?

multi-task." I guess that would be the ultimate in multi-tasking. It's amazing how far we've come—welcome to the world of technology.

So, is it improper? You better answer quickly, this isn't gonna wait!

Never mind, I gotta go; I'll talk to you tomorrow.

what about miracles and other "signs from god?"

We've all heard of these events, haven't we? Some are more spectacular (and in some cases more unbelievable) than others. This part of the book is about where they come from.

Hey, I gotta stop here and say something: Merry Christmas!

It's Christmas morning 2007 and I'm here on my laptop (don't worry, I'm at the kitchen table) before anyone gets up. I woke up at around four and couldn't go back to sleep, so I figured I'd get up, pour a hot cup and sit down with you. Sorry if there are more typos here—I'm typing in the dark.

I wish my flashlight had batteries.

Am I the only one who feels this? Have you ever stayed awake on Christmas Eve, after everyone else is asleep, or have you ever awakened hours before anyone else on Christmas morning? Isn't there a special feeling in the silence? On this night in particular? Maybe it's just me, but I remember working Christmas Eve nights driving around my district at two or three in the morning. I couldn't explain it then, and I can't articulate it now.

That's a big word—articulate—isn't it? I remember learning it in Mr. Parker's class. It means: *To express in coherent verbal form; give words to*. Me being the smart-ass that I was (and still am??), I wrote down this definition of *articulate* on a vocab test: "*Although I know what this word means, I'm having difficulty putting the definition into words*." Thank God Mr. Parker had a sense of humor—no phone call home! Just another *D* to add to my resume.

Have you ever had that feeling? The one where you know what you're thinking but can't get the words out of your mouth? Yeah, me too. That's the same feeling that I'm feeling now. There's a calmness on this night that is unlike any other night. A sense of peace; a sense of security that says, "Everything is going to be okay." All the presents are wrapped, all the decorations are up—maybe it's exhaustion?! Whatever it is, don't you wish you could have this feeling all year long? Exactly how I feel.

I can go back in time and pick that feeling out of my memory on the nights I was alone in my patrol car (sometimes fighting to stay awake) driving around on Christmas Eve. Our shifts are 12-hour shifts, which means you work 7 a.m. to7 p.m., or 7 p.m. to 7 a.m..

On those Christmas Eves when I was working nights, I had the opportunity to see all the decorations on the houses in my district, all the lights, scenes and displays. You wanna know what I didn't see a lot of? Nativity scenes. Just a few scattered here and there, just like last night (2007).

Driving home from church last night (I go more than two times a year now, honest—I swear to God) I saw the same number of Nativity scenes. Although now they're a lot more elaborate than in the 80s and 90s. I saw this one in particular with a spotlight on it. Not only was the manger scene done tastefully, this homeowner took the time to hang a large light, in the shape of a star, over the manger. It was hung from a pole that was attached to a tree behind the manger. That was really creative.

Back to driving around on Christmas Eve. It was just a feeling that made the time go faster and that "feeling sorry for myself" attitude of having to work on Christmas Eve got a little better. Watching the interior lights in houses go off, one by one, as I drove around was something that made me stop and wonder: Were the people in each of those houses going to wake up to a good Christmas? Were the kids going to get everything they wanted?

And the question that I could never answer: Why did I have this *feeling* on this night? The feeling I could never *articulate*. I've worked a lot of nights. Why on this night did that feeling make everything seem okay? Why on this night did I park my patrol car, roll down the window, turn off the engine, and then just listen? The silence of this night is magical. Why?

And why do we still call it "rolling down a car window?" All I did was push a button on the armrest and down it went. I think we should come up with a new term for lowering a car window.

can i get there from here?

That's it: *lowering*! I lowered the car window. It's amazing, isn't it? How we hold on to old habits, to old sayings? I had a habit of only going to church twice a year, how about you?

Well, it's time to make breakfast and get coffee going for everyone else. I'll get back to you later tonight—if I'm still awake! In the meantime, have a great Christmas and enjoy the "reason for the season."

How was your Christmas? I hope you were blessed with everything you wanted, and everything you wanted to give to your loved ones. I wanted, or should I say need, a GPS for my car. Didn't get it. Maybe next year ...

Today was one of those days that just flew by. Gifts, breakfast, more gifts, lunch, visits with family/visits to family, snacks, more gifts, dinner, dessert (my favorite meal of the day if you're asking), late-night sandwiches, more dessert (still my favorite); throw in a half-gallon or so of coffee throughout the day, and wow!

At least I was able to take a few minutes and remember the reason for this day. With all the hustle and bustle, it's hard to take time for ourselves, don't ya think? I also remember that on this day, a couple thousand of years ago, a miracle took place. And since we're on the topic of miracles, I thought, why not start with this one.

What do you think the chances are that I would be at this place in this book on this day? Think about it, I started this book shortly after Thanksgiving (motivation—what a great gift) and have been hacking away at it day and night. I've been adding chapters/sections as I go and as I think of them. So I had no idea, as I shared with you on the outset, where this book was going to take us. I still have no idea how it's gonna end.

Nothing's changed since then—with the exception of the cat. He killed a mouse the other day and left it in the kitchen as a present for us. Did you ever get a frantic phone call where you believe there's a life-or-death emergency that requires you to drive there at Mach-two speed? What a letdown (at least for cops, firefighters and other emergency service workers) to find a dead mouse on the kitchen floor! Another story for another book...

Back to the point I'm trying to make (sorry—it's probably the eggnog talking). To start something, with no real direction, and find yourself at a point where you're talking about miracles is something. But to arrive at this point in time, at this point in the book, on Christmas Day. No way! Yeah, it really is Christmas Day—2007. The Eagles won last Sunday—they beat the Saints in New Orleans, thirty-eight to twenty-three.

What do you think the chances are that I'd be writing this page, on this subject, at this time, on this day? Perhaps *another* Christmas miracle? I'll let you ponder that while I go fill my last eggnog of the night.

———————

Have you ever burped up eggnog? More Tums, please.

I have no idea what the first recorded miracle was, but I do have an idea of what the most significant miracle in history is. Yep, you guessed it—Christmas and everything that leads up to it. To avoid arguments, let's review. There is a God, a God who knows and loves each and every one of us. He sent his Son to us to not only teach us, but most impor-

can i get there from here?

tantly, to save us. That Son, Jesus, was crucified for our sins so that we could have eternal life.

And what about his birth? The miracle of birth; the miracle of *this* birth—a virgin gave birth to Jesus.

How many miracles are in the Christmas Story?

Let's start with the conception; how about Joseph and Mary deciding to name their child Jesus on the advice of an angel, then Jesus being born on a cold night and surviving in a manger, and fleeing into Egypt to avoid "The Massacre of the Innocent" on the advice of yet another angel?

For me, Christmas is a time of self-reflection. I look at my own life and then think of his life. My beginnings weren't as humble as his (I was born in a hospital), and my life certainly won't leave an impression on the world like his did. I don't want to start comparing myself to others, but every now and then—especially at Christmas—I find myself wondering: could I ever be as good a person as Jesus was? Of all the things I complain about and all the things I get upset over, why is it at this time of the year I wonder why? Why do I complain about what I don't have, then bitch and moan when I get something I didn't want or didn't ask for? And how come I get upset at the littlest things that really won't make a bit of difference in my life the next day?

On this day, it really is a miracle that we all find ourselves a little more relaxed (after the presents are opened) and a little more forgiving. Maybe we shouldn't be looking for the super-duper miracles that we read about or see on TV. Maybe we're supposed to see the everyday miracles, and especially today, appreciate the miracle of life—the life of Jesus.

Let me leave you with this until tomorrow:

But the angel said to them, "Do not be afraid. I bring you good news of great joy that will be for all the people. Today in the town of David a Savior has been born to you; he is Christ the Lord. This will be a sign to you: You will find a baby wrapped in cloths and lying in a manger."

Luke, Chapter 2, Verses 10–12 (NIV)

Angels—miracles or subplots for movies and television shows? Beats me, I never met one. Yeah I did—and I asked her to marry me this past Thanksgiving. Pretty romantic, don't ya think? How could she say no? Trust me; I knew what I was doing there.

Are we all waiting for a miracle to happen before we act? That's what a lot of us do, don't you agree? We sit around waiting for some sign, some miracle that will somehow give us the motivation we are looking for. What is a miracle, anyway? I bet I can Google it before you find it on Dictionary.com!

Told you I'd beat you; here it is: "... derived from the old Latin word *miraculum* meaning 'something wonderful'..." Thank you, Wikipedia. This is just one of many parts of the definition. But do you remember the KISS Principle? Keeping it simple—*something wonderful*. The definition continues with words like divine intervention and overruled course and operation of nature ...

Fine, I'll give you that. But let's keep it simple, okay? There are a whole bunch of miracles documented in the Bible. Here's a couple:

can i get there from here?

Miracle in the Old Testament: Moses parting the Sea of Reeds (Red Sea).

Miracle in the New Testament: Jesus turning water into wine and turning one loaf of bread into many loaves.

This isn't a book on the Bible, remember, so that's all I'm adding. I put miracles here just to point out that they happened. And we know they happened because it says so in the Bible, and we just agreed in the last chapter that the Bible is accurate.

But what about other miracles; you know, the ones that happen to *real* people—like you and me?

All right, here's proof. All those people abducted by aliens! The miracle isn't that they were abducted, but that they survived the alien anal probes and were returned to earth to be reunited with their families. That's a miracle! I'm sorry if I offended any UFO nuts (sorry again for that slanderous description) by the previous sarcastic statement. I'm just joking, remember? We're not going to start taking ourselves too seriously, are we?

Do you want to know what David Hume said about miracles? First you probably want to know who David Hume is—well actually, *was*. Hume was an eighteenth-century Scottish philosopher considered among the most important figures in the history of Western Philosophy and the Scottish Enlightenment. If you Google Hume (that almost sounds vulgar) you'd see that Hume was also considered one of the biggest skeptics of his time—especially when it came to religion, specifically Christianity. Many labeled Hume as an atheist. It wasn't until just weeks before he died that he confided in a friend that *he sincerely believed it a "most unreasonable fancy" that there might be life after death*. What was Hume trying to say there? Was he suggesting although in his mind it was unreasonable, that there could be life after death? He used the word fancy, as if to describe a possibility? When someone is on his deathbed, words and thoughts can get confused. Perhaps Hume had a change of heart at the last minute?

Now that you know him, here's a part of what Hume had to say about miracles: *A miracle is "a transgression of a law of nature by a particular volition of the Deity, or by the interposition of some invisible agent."*

Hume would go on to argue, *"Miracles have a very low probability of occurring."* Yet, facing death, Hume acknowledges his belief in something he touted for years to be impossible: *life after death.* Is that a miracle, life after death? Think about it, death means just that—dead (I checked it out on ask.com). How can anything live after it is dead? Perhaps Hume had a change of thought at the last minute. It's never too late, is it?

I mentioned Hume for a reason. There's a quick anecdote about him which I have often quoted. I've used it when talking about men of character and integrity. The story goes something like this:

Hume's friends used to tease him for going to church every Sunday to hear his minister preach. Hume silenced his friends with this. "Well," he told them, "I don't believe everything he says, but he lives what he believes. And once a week I like to hear a man who believes what he says."

Even the most skeptical philosopher of the 18th century went to church on Sundays. A miracle, perhaps?

And speaking of miracles, I almost forgot to tell you about a Christmas present I got as a kid. Can you guess what grade I was in? It was either fifth or sixth, I'm not sure. Why was fifth grade such a turning point in my life? The first decade

can i get there from here?

of my life was relatively uneventful. Then, eleven years old and bam (tribute to Emeril)!

Anyway, my brother Glenn and I wanted a chemistry set for Christmas; and I think my mom had to talk my dad into it. Christmas morning came and I couldn't believe what I saw. This thing had all kinds of chemicals (just what a kid like me needed) and instructions (what a kid like me didn't need) that were supposed to teach you how to perform different experiments. It even had a card listing all the safety rules, but my brother threw that out with the wrapping paper. As for the instructions, we knew what we were doing, and they looked boring anyway.

As you read this, think of "The Fourth of July in December." Go ahead, close your eyes and picture a Fourth of July fireworks display on a cold winter day...

So we go out in the backyard and start pouring all the different colored chemicals together in a beaker that came with the set. The way Glenn and I figured it the beaker was meant to be filled to the top. That's why they made it that size (perfect logic—don't you think). This chemistry set didn't come with anything capable of producing a flame, so we had to sneak into the house and steal my parents' matches. Back out in the yard—just me and my brother. All of the company was inside staying warm. I don't know what the names of the chemicals were that we put in the beaker, but when gently stirred, they combined to form a pale yellow color. Now came the time for the experiment, in two stages.

Here are the steps we performed this experiment, in the exact order they were performed:

- Take one children's chemistry set
- Pour portions of every chemical into a glass beaker
- Stir or shake gently
- Procure an ignition source
- Ignite beaker
- Run like hell!

The second stage of this experiment included putting out whatever was still burning in the backyard; including your brother—if he's still on fire.

No belt that time, just the memory of my dad and uncle running out the back door, each holding a fire extinguisher. Remember, I said my mom had to talk my dad into getting it for us. Well, I say that because of the comments made *by* my dad, *to* my mom, *about* us after the carnage had been examined by family and neighbors who had witnessed the fireball. Suffice it to say, dad didn't think we were mature enough to handle a chemistry set.

Back then, dad didn't know what he was talking about. It wasn't until Glenn and I got out of high school that we realized his real intelligence and concern for us. Isn't that a shame? We spend our teenage years doing everything we can to get away from our parents. We take their advice as nagging, or "stop telling me what to do!" Once we get older, we go back and try to become their friends. Is it a miracle that our parents take us back into their hearts when *we're* ready for it? Am I the only one who said some pretty crappy things to my parents? And even after saying and doing all the stuff I did, they still had open hearts for me when I got old enough to understand their caring and concern. My father had so

can i get there from here?

much concern for us that he took what was left of the chemistry set and hid it from us until he could throw it away.

If dad was so smart, why would he hide the chemistry set in the same place he hid the presents the week before? Glenn and I figured he put it there for us to find. Wanna know what we did when my parents went back to work the next day? We found the chemistry set in his closet (along with a couple of Playboys—dad, I'm so disappointed) and took it back to the scene of the crime. There were still enough chemicals left for our next experiment. By the way, if this ever went to court, my brother and I were covered. Even though she was screaming and saying the rosary when she ran out of the house yesterday, mom never said not to make anymore experiments. And dad never directly told us not to look for the chemistry set, and he also did not specifically tell us not to do anymore experiments. He just yelled, and yelled at Glenn and me some more; then he yelled at my mom, "Jeanne, I need a Manhattan!"

Manhattan—2 parts Scotch to 1 part sweet Vermouth, add ice and stir. Cough syrup tastes better! But that wouldn't stop Glenn and me from sneaking sips from dad's Manhattan as the years went on. Note to anyone who hasn't had a Manhattan: It is a drink meant to be sipped—not chugged! And if your father had the same habits as mine, make sure his hands are clean. Dad would sit in his chair holding his Manhattan with one hand while he stirred the ice with the pinkie finger of his other hand.

Just a friendly reminder as a public service to the readers of this book.

Back to December twenty-sixth. This wasn't an experiment. Rather, it would be a rocket launch.

Here are the steps we performed for this endeavor:

- Take one cardboard paper towel roll
- Use masking tape to seal-off one end
- Poke a string through the middle of the masking tape
- Fill the bottom third of the tube (main rocket booster) with match heads
- *(nothing good is going to come from this, is it?)*
- Fill the remaining portion of the tube with available chemicals not destroyed in the conflagration from the previous day (NASA calls this the fuel cell)
- Roll top of rocket into a point for aerodynamic efficiency
- Mount rocket to bicycle spoke pointing skyward
- Find parents' matches
- Announce official countdown—ten, nine, eight...
- Talk your younger brother into igniting the string
- Run like hell (again)

No fire ball this time. The matches didn't have the pressure-oxygen ratio necessary to explode—they just burned. Had we used aluminum foil instead of the cardboard (as was learned in future experiments... er... launches), then we would've had something. The chemicals just smoldered, forming a huge plume of smoke. Basically, my brother and I built a big smoke bomb. We were disappointed that nothing went into the sky, but we were also still alive!

So, what do you think about miracles so far? Why did I just take up a couple of valuable pages of this book to enlighten you a little more about my delinquent past? Well, think about this. Should my brother and I still be here today? One experiment on Christmas Day that should have taken our heads off, and a failed rocket launch the following day that should have just blown up. Who or what intervened to cause, as David Hume would say, *a transgression of a law of nature*? Can you imagine running out of your house on Christmas Day to see your kids dead in the backyard? Me either! We should have been dead.

I bet if we could go back and find all the chemicals in that kit, and then find a science teacher willing to explain what would happen if you put all of them together and lit them on fire, we'd agree that my brother and I should have been dead. If I could have taken a picture of the backyard, you would also agree that there was no way we should have walked away from that. And what about our rocket ship? The day after Christmas and we still didn't learn our lesson. After spending the last twenty-two years of my life as a cop, and the four years prior to that as a paramedic, I can tell you I've seen the tragic results of some of these experiments gone wrong.

During my tenure as a cop, I also was a canine handler with a bomb dog—a big bouncy rambunctious black Labrador Retriever named Boomer (my kids' idea). In that role I had the opportunity to work with bomb technicians who shared with me some of their insights. Did you know that match heads are used to make some very powerful pipe bombs? Yep, just match heads.

Back to our rocket ship. We could have reached for the Reynolds's Wrap, but instead we took the paper towel roll. Why? If we would have wrapped the match heads in aluminum foil, real tight like kids like to wrap things, it would have been disastrous. Guaranteed, no questions. Trust me, we made small miniature rocket ships in the months that followed, and they were out of aluminum foil—with just a couple match heads in them. And boy did they fly! Can you imagine what a couple hundred match heads would do? Uh, I don't know if there were any witnesses to *that event* in my freshman year of high school, so I refuse to answer that question on the grounds I might incriminate myself. But trust me on this, it makes a *big* bang.

So why are my brother and I still here? Back then we chalked it up to dumb luck. But looking back at it now, could it have been a miracle? Why do miracles have to be grand to be believed? Can't the little things that happen in life also be miracles? Who's to say that God didn't intervene back on those cold December days? Does he always have to make a magnificent entrance? Do you remember our *simple* definition of miracle?

Something Wonderful

Do you think my mom and dad thought it was something wonderful that they still had their two children? Two children, by the way, who as their mom would say *numerous* times—didn't have the brains that God gave ants! Yeah, I bet mom and dad thought it was wonderful, especially after dad's third Manhattan that afternoon.

How about you? Has anything like this ever happened in your life, either to you or someone you know? Was it dumb luck after all? Or maybe, just maybe, a small miracle took place. A miracle that is there for us to see, if we really look for it. Some of us say "Someone was looking out for us." Yep, I agree! Who is he? Maybe angels really do exist.

can i get there from here?

As far as miracles, it's a miracle my brother and I were never arrested...make that convicted. After the chemistry set calamity, my parents got us a telescope the following year. We were both a year older and a year wiser. Maybe too wise. A telescope is used to check out the moon, observe the stars and explore our galaxy. Not for us. We used it to check out a college student one street over from our house. She was home for Christmas break (I think colleges are still permitted to say Christmas) and she would get undressed in her bedroom at the same time every night. Lights on in the bedroom, curtains open; what more could a couple of adolescent boys want?

My parents were so happy: we couldn't blow anything up with the telescope! And they let us take it to the *ball field* every night after dinner to watch the stars—and moon (ten easy points for the moon reference). The only problem: Images in the telescope were upside down! When you looked through a telescope back then, the image you saw was upside down. Those images in the window took a toll later in high school when I got into arguments with my sex education teacher about the anatomical position of different body parts. Anyone ever try running from the police carrying a telescope and tripod? Enough said.

So what about these little signs from God (someone who was looking out for us), the ones we ignore for the most part? Are they there for us to read as if they're signs along a highway? Think about it; how many times have you said to yourself: "I *knew* that was going to happen"? You had a gut feeling before you did it, didn't you? We've all had that gut feeling. Some women call it a premonition. You know, a woman's intuition. Why did God give them all the good stuff?

What if we assume that life is an interstate, and each of our individual lives are the cars we're driving to our destination. Simple enough so far, right? Think about those caution signs, speed limit signs, information signs, and even the mile markers. Can we make an analogy of this scenario with our personal lives? By this point in my life, I can make *anything* an analogy! So here we are, driving down the highway of life.

I'm not sure if I'd be driving a Hummer or BMW. I like the power and muscle of the Hummer, yet the Beemer has something exciting to it. They both offer something different that I want; damn it, another perplexing decision. Don't you wish life was simple, like only one car manufacturer? Then we'd all be driving the same thing. Great, my luck would have us all driving a Yugo! Anyone remember that little piece of automotive innovation?

Where were we going with this (ten points for the innuendo *going* in reference to driving down life's highway)? Okay, we're on life's superhighway on our destination to...That's another thing; where are we going? What is our final destination? Maybe another subject for another book. Let's stay focused with this one.

We're on our highway, and our trip is going one of three ways. It's *going great*—car's running fine, weather is good, little or no traffic; *going okay*—car will need gas soon, it's starting to rain, and traffic is slowing a little bit; *it sucks*—this rental car is piece of crap, the air-conditioning is broken, an accident in the middle of rush-hour traffic has caused a standstill, and it's snowing. Anyone's life come to mind? How many times do we go from great to okay to sucky and then back again?

Some days we notice the signs along the way. And

depending on our day, we might actually pay attention to them. But what if we're distracted or were looking for something else, or we're so preoccupied with our destination that we forget to see the things along the way? The signs are still there, aren't they? But we missed them. Even though all the other drivers saw them and paid attention, we curse and blame the engineers who thought of this stupid traffic pattern. You know, the morons who made these signs so friggin small no one could see them, and of course, anyone who was in the car with us that made us miss the sign.

It's our car, we're in the driver's seat, but it's someone else's fault. Am I the only one who's experienced this phenomenon? Let's say we wanted to get off at a particular exit and we're looking for the exit sign. We want to get off at Exit 132. We are having a good day today (for a change) and have the radio tuned to our favorite song—something from Mr. Jimmy Buffet for me. Our thoughts start to wander, and before we know it we're passing Exit 138. " ... *wastin' away again in Margaritaville, searching for my...* " What happened? How could this happen to me, *again*?

I'll tell you how. We just missed the signs along the way. Simple as that. KISS. Yep, the exit sign was there the entire time. We were just too busy, too distracted, too preoccupied, or too lazy to recognize it—even if we were looking for it the whole time. That sounds crazy doesn't it? How can we miss something that's right there in front of us if we're looking for it? Easy, our brain is conditioned—programmed, if you will—to disregard the stuff that it doesn't think it will need or can't use because there's something else more important to think about.

How about trying something to see if I'm right? But you have to promise not to cheat!

Okay, here goes. When I tell you, turn the page and read the entire sentence *one time*. As you read, count to yourself how many times the letter *f* is used in the sentence. That's simple enough, right? But you have to promise me—actually promise yourself—that you won't cheat and reread the sentence. Honest, this will all make sense (I hope) later.

Okay, turn the page and read the sentence; count the *f*s as you're reading, then turn to the next page.

Finished files are the result of years of scientific study combined with the experience of the years.

Okay, you promise you didn't cheat? How many *f*s did you count?

Did you see *three f*s?

Don't go back and check!

Did you see *four f*s?

Don't you dare go back and reread the sentence!

Did you see *five f*s?

Temptation is an evil; don't even think about it!

Who saw all *six f*s?

Okay, now you can go back and reread the sentence to see if I'm crazy. Go ahead, I'll wait...

What happened?

Here's what happened and, yes, there are really six *f*s. As we read—as we observe (as in the highway exit sign analogy)—we discount things that don't matter. Or we go back to our old habits or ways of thinking and we don't see the obvious. When we read the sentence and get to the word *of*, we pronounce it as *uv*; u-v in our brain. Our brain knows what the word is, but because we pronounce it *uv*, we miss the *f* in the word *of*. Conditioned observations—discounting things that really aren't important.

Who got all six? Good for you. How about the rest of *us*? This isn't an IQ test; finding a letter has nothing to do with intelligence. It deals with observation. Pretty cool—unless you saw this before and now you're bored and rolling your eyes. Sorry, *Mr. I Know Everything*; I'll try to come up with something more challenging for you later.

I put all that out there for this summation. Our highway of life is a super highway with a lot of signs, exits, and sometimes, detours. But mainly signs. Depending on the day we're having (great, okay, or sucky) and other factors (distractions, preoccupations, hobbies), we either see the signs along the road, or we miss them. And even if we see them, we might not pay attention to them because we're *conditioned* not to read them.

The highway is the human race; our car is our life and we're in the driver's seat; there are signs (gut feelings, premonitions, intuitions) all along the road—the road of life. Now a question: Who put the signs all along the road? Were they dropped there arbitrarily; or did they just happen to land in the right place, as in the Big Bang Theory? Or were they placed along the road, our highway of life, by someone who wanted us to pay attention to them? Is it a miracle that they're there for us to read, observe, and take notice of? What if we took notice of them more often? How much better could our lives be?

Is it a miracle when we do actually read them, or when we do see all six *f*s? The *f*s were there all along. Weren't they? Just like the signs along our highway; they've been there all along, positioned and posted by *the* supreme traffic engineer who knew just where to place them to make sure we saw our exit. This supreme traffic engineer knew what mile post to place them, which exit signs would mean the most to us, what caution signs would do us the most good, and what colors to use to get our attention. And only he knows where this highway is leading and where the end of the road is.

So, would it be a miracle if we just enjoyed the ride along this super highway of life, instead of trying to figure out where this highway is taking us? What if we trusted the supreme traffic engineer who laid this road out for us in the first place? And what if we had *faith* in him, enough faith to take our time and read the signs? The signs are there for a reason, aren't they?

Can you imagine if we did take our time—to enjoy the view, to enjoy the company; to enjoy the scenery, and to appreciate the work that was done to keep this highway safe for us? It always was in safe hands.

That would be "*Something Wonderful.*"

Miracles—they're there for everyone. They can't be explained by scientific reason, so we tend to discount them (*poo-poo them* for the intellectual reader). Or the probability of something miraculous happening is so small that we call it luck when it happens. Like the right person, one out of only 3,500 in the world, being there for a needed project. Can we use that figure for this part? I wanted to wrap this chapter up with a story that's real. Something that I got to see firsthand.

But first, I wanted to let you know that I did look-up the word "awesomest." Remember way back in the chapter: *Whose idea was it to send Jesus to earth?* I told you I didn't know if it was a word. Well I just got around to checking it out, and sure enough, it's not a word. Now I'm stuck. Do I go back and change it, or leave it there? If I go back and change it, you would never know it was there in the first place, would you? Because, and follow my logic here, if I leave it you would know it was there when you read it the first time. But if I go back and change it now, then it would have never been there for you to read when you bought this book (thank you again) in the first place. And then all of this rambling would have been for nothing. I guess I'll keep awesomest in there so all this makes sense.

Back to the little miracle I saw unfold first hand. Last summer, my fiancée and I joined a small community church in the small town where I live (part of my return to faith). To give you perspective, the church is one of the original log buildings in this community of only one square mile. The church has beauty beyond explanation, and couples (including a *couple* famous ones) from hundreds of miles away have come to this church to get married. It's modest and quaint, with perhaps one hundred fifty to two hundred people at each Sunday service.

Imagine how many different professions/trades/expertise are represented by the congregation, maybe a doctor or two, a half-dozen teachers, some administrative assistants (I learned, they're not secretaries), a handful of contractors—you get the picture. Not like a large church with parking for five-hundred cars! And although not a true Congregationalist Church, there are committees and bylaws and all that kind of stuff. Some of the committees are larger than others, but one in particular, Mission Council (which my fiancée and I are now members of), is a committee that decides where donations will be spent for those in need (food, clothing, housing, and medical care to name a few). It has about ten to twelve members. Over this past summer, members of the congregation were speaking with another member about the plight of his family in Sierra Leone. He is a United States citizen and he immigrated here years ago. But his family is still there—and they have no potable water in their village. That's right, no wells for drinking water. Sickness is common among the children and clean water would go a long way to combat some of the diseases which plague the village. So what does Mission Council do? They decide to build a well in Sierra Leone. Half-a-globe away and these people are going to get a well built for a member's former village. Yeah, right...Look, if they were able to pull it off, that would be a miracle in and of itself. But it gets better.

As they began to research this project—cost analysis, logistical concerns, and financial constraints, it became obvious that no one on the committee knew anything about drilling a well. Everywhere they turned they were faced with new challenges—*hurdles*—not roadblocks. And one that kept coming back and seemed insurmountable was their lack of knowledge in the planning of the well—its position, depth, material, and, of course, a small little detail of its location so they would hit water! They needed a Hydrogeologist, and these guys were hard to find. There is an association of them—it's the International Association of Hydrogeologists, or IAH for short. Go ahead, you probably want to check this out. That'll give me time to put the dogs out. I'll be back.

Did you find it? Yeah, I told you—it really does exist. Who knew? I didn't even know there was such a thing as a Hydrogeologist, did you? No one on Mission Council knew they existed either...until they had another monthly meeting. And at this meeting a member showed up who had been absent from the previous meetings where the well project was discussed. As they were pondering the fate of the well, a member spoke up. She asked, "You need a what? A Hy-dro-ge-ol-o-gist?" The members then took turns explaining that without one, this project—the church's dream of supplying clean drinking water to this village—would have to be squashed. Remember, it's the responsibility of the Mission Council to

can i get there from here?

determine where money from donations and requests gets allocated. This woman then announced that her husband is in the business—he was a certified and licensed Hydrogeologist.

You tell me the odds of that! A small little church in a small little community with a Hydrogeologist in its congregation. I say that because, according to their web site, the International Association of Hydrogeologists has three thousand five hundred members in one hundred thirty-five countries. Compare that to the American Medical Association which has more than six hundred fifty thousand members just in the United States, and to the AFL-CIO which has a little more than 10 million members in this country.

What are the odds of a Hydrogeologist (one out of three thousand five hundred in the world) being a member of our church? And take that further—what are the chances that his wife would be on the committee that would need him? Add to that the odds of an immigrant from Sierra Leone moving to our community and joining this church—the same church with the Hydrogeologist who is married to a woman on the Mission Council? This kind of thing is just what God wants us to see. It's why God wants us to scratch our heads and say, "How does he do it?" It's these small little miracles that start to add up. Not the ones where the news cameras are there to capture the little girl being saved from the jaws of some horrific death by an unbelievable chain of events. Yeah they happen, and thank God they do. But what about a well—costing four thousand U.S. dollars—for a village in a country torn by war, poverty, corruption and who knows what else? This country is so far away that most of us couldn't find it on a globe. And yet, a small community in New Jersey had a dream of making sure a village a world away had clean drinking water. And that dream was fulfilled in January of 2008 when the well became operational.

Our church held a party and the member whose family is still in Sierra Leone couldn't believe what had happened. And *none* of it would have happened if one church member didn't go to a meeting on one certain night of the week. And *none* of it would have happened if that same church member didn't marry a man who was a Hy-dro-ge-ol-o-gist.

A "*Miracle*" or just "*Something Wonderful*"? For the people in that village in Sierra Leone, does it really matter what it's called?

Hey, before we go onto the next chapter, I'd like to share something else with you, and I'd like to get your thoughts. I've mentioned numerous times in this book the impact some of my teachers had on me. There were a lot of teachers who believed in me—who had *faith* in me. Even though I was a pain in the ass in their class, they didn't give up on me.

Isn't that cool? Someone who refuses to give up on you, who has *faith* in you, even though you're a pain in the ass? These kinds of people are pretty special. Imagine a kind of supreme traffic engineer who has that kind of faith in people and who refuses to give up on us. Back to the everyday people who make a difference in other people's lives—teachers. We all know them because no matter what your age, occupation, experience, or income, we all have been impacted by teachers. Some of those encounters were good, and others, well—not so good. Whose fault was that?

I'll be the first to admit it; there are some good people out there and some not-so-good people out there. And they don't change when they go to work. Anyone out there ever been given a speeding ticket? How about being treated unfairly by a cop? Yeah, even good cops have bad days. And there are cops that I wouldn't want to have over for dinner either. So we agree that there are good people—those who try to do the right thing, those who try to help others, and there are not-so-good people out there—those who have a negative impact on our lives, those who appear to take enjoyment out of other people's misfortunes. It's the same with teachers. Some connect with kids and some shouldn't be in a classroom. Same can be said of doctors and hospitals (we all have horror stories about doctors and hospitals—yet when we're sick, where do we go?).

I didn't have a choice—I had to go to school. How about you? Were you able to stay home when you wanted, or miss the classes that were taught by teachers you didn't like? I told you from the beginning you and me were a lot alike!

Teachers who should have given up on me didn't—for some reason. My gym teacher, Mr. Burtis, kicked me in the ass (literally) to get me to straighten-up. He told me he wasn't going to let me get away with the same stuff I pulled on my other teachers. He very easily could have just ignored my wise-ass comments, sent me to the office, or given me an F. I would have deserved any and all of them. But you know what he did instead? He got me interested in weight lifting and working out. In other words, doing something good for myself—something that would have a positive effect. Within a year I competed in the school's weight-lifting competition and came in first in the bench press. Not bad for a kid who spent most of the time in the office! I had the school record for the bench press in my weight class for a year, only a year. Nothing lasts forever!

Mr. Burtis was one of the numerous teachers who didn't give up on me. Even Mr. Morgan, my high school disciplinarian—I don't think he gave up on me either. I was job security for him. But imagine the surprised look on the faces of the teachers who did give up on me? Six years later, I walked back into the school for a call for service. There were no resource officers then—if the school needed a cop, they called the police department and asked for one to be sent. I still remember walking into the office and getting chills when I looked at the seats where you sat until the principal was ready to call you into his office. Some memories die hard...

The principal saw me, looked at my uniform—official badge and real gun (with bullets)—and began looking around for the hidden video cameras. He thought he was being set-up on Candid Camera. His first words: "No way, you can't be a police officer!" Yep, I was. He grabbed me, gave me a hug and said, "Congratulations." He was proud of me. I guess the word spread in school because by the time I left (I don't remember the nature of the call) teachers were hanging out in front of the office just to get a glimpse of me. Even the ladies in the office (I can say that, can't I?) were amazed. They were the ones who let me use their phone to call my mom the last day of school to let her know I was going to be walking in the graduation ceremony later that night.

How does that equate with miracles? Well first of all, I know the teachers were thinking of God my last day of school. Most could be overheard saying, "Thank God he's out of here." They really were proud of me—they even gave

can i get there from here?

thanks to God. But the ones who didn't give up on me, the ones who wouldn't let me give up on myself—they were the real miracle workers. If not for them (especially Mr. Parker and Mr. Burtis), I wouldn't be where I am today. My only regret? Why didn't I pay more attention in the science and math classes? Listening to a lecture on anatomy and physiology in paramedic school was hard … cell structure, biology of the human body, drug and body weight calculations. Why didn't I pay attention in chemistry, biology, and algebra? Sitting there having no idea what they were talking about—that was challenging, perhaps even a *hurdle* in my way to getting where I wanted to go.

After high school, what sign was there for me to go from wanting to become an Episcopal priest to a paramedic to a cop? Gut feelings, intuitions, hunches (cops have a lot of them)? I don't know. But they—forks in the superhighway of life—were laid out in front of me. And there were signs along the way that led me to different exits, in different directions. Looking back, I must have paid attention to the signs along the way—along the way to my destination. Beats me where I'll end up—kind of like this book—but I'm going to enjoy the ride on my way!

If I didn't follow the signs in my life, I wouldn't be here right now. I wouldn't have had the life experiences needed to write this, and to become the person I am today. I guess I must have had faith in the traffic engineer who guided me here. What about you? Have you ever looked back and wondered why you took the paths you did?

What do you say we move on to the next chapter?

why do bad
things happen to
good people?

Here are excerpts from some letters, all written by the same person that I would like to share with you:

"I am told God lives in me—and yet the reality of darkness and coldness and emptiness is so great that nothing touches my soul."

"Darkness is such that I really do not see—neither with my mind nor with my reason—the place of God in my soul is blank. There is no God in me—when the pain of longing is so great—I just long & long for God.... The torture and pain I can't explain."

"In my soul, I can't tell you how dark it is, how painful, how terrible—I feel like refusing God."

"Today, I wandered the streets the whole day. My feet are aching and I have not been able to find a home. And I also get the temptation, of the tempter telling me, 'Leave all this'…"

"If I ever become a Saint—I will surely be one of 'darkness.'" "I will continually be absent from Heaven—to (light) the light of those in darkness on earth."

Any guesses?

This person wrote these letters starting in the early 60s. This person would start a mission that would feed five hundred thousand families a year, treat ninety thousand leprosy patients annually, and educate twenty thousand children every year.

"Where I try to raise my thoughts to heaven, there is such convicting emptiness that those very thoughts return like sharp knives and hurt my very soul. Love—the word—it brings nothing," also wrote the woman known the world over as the *Messiah of Love*.

Did you get it yet?

It's Mother Theresa!

How could this Nobel Peace Prize winning nun (who will probably be named a saint) have these feelings? How could she have these feelings as she conducted her ministries? Boy, talk about doubt!

I can't think of one person—not even David Hume—who could find something negative to say about Mother Theresa. In fact, when you speak of her, nothing but praise comes to mind. And yet, this true gentle woman, who gave up everything to walk the slums of Calcutta, was tormented by these thoughts. Fear, doubt, anguish, misery, and pain. Why?

Because that's the only way it can be. Doesn't it make sense that if we are free to express ourselves, free to love who we want, even free to take chances on a crazy lottery scheme, then we have to have *Total* freedom? Some might argue that it's God's plan. Maybe, maybe not. The only one who knows for sure is God. Anyone care to ask him what he's doing up there? How about giving the big guy some pointers on how he could do it better—you know, the way we would do it. With the exception of some pretty good movies and some pretty not-so-good movies, God hasn't told anyone why he does what he does.

By the way, I can't be the only one who thought *Bruce Almighty* was funny. That movie proved beyond a shadow of a doubt how screwed-up the world would get if God let one of us take the reins for a little while. Come on, who wouldn't make Jennifer Aniston's chest bigger if they had a chance? What, you mean *Bruce Almighty* wasn't a documentary on the second coming of the Lord?

Nah, *Bruce Almighty* was just a Hollywood writer's idea of what could happen if God gave his powers to a man. But can you think of the problems that could cause? Whoever got to take the job over, even for a week, would be hounded

can i get there from here?

by calls from his or her friends. Can you imagine the requests for favors? We've all read about those horror stories about people whose lives were ruined after winning the lottery. That was only a couple of hundred million dollars and these people had to change their identity to avoid being robbed or killed. Can you imagine what would happen if someone found out you were God—even for a single day?

The phone calls and e-mails from people claiming to be your friends, visits from cousins you never knew existed, and families of sick people in your neighborhood begging for you to perform a miracle on a loved one. And what about the requests for favors? How much temptation could one person take? Where would he or she draw the line in what they offered and what they didn't? Maybe *Bruce Almighty* was a documentary after all? But not *Something about Mary*! Two movies that were funnier than anything, but two movies that could never be confused with imitating the other.

Why did I compare *Bruce Almighty* to *Something About Mary*? I don't know—I saw both of them on HBO in recent weeks. Maybe it's because I took two Alka Seltzer Plus Night Time Cold tablets twenty minutes ago and I feel like my head is spinning. It was pounding; now it's spinning. Even if you're not a doctor, you can probably figure out what I got: fever, chills, body aches, stuffy nose, cough, pounding headache (now spinning), nausea, and a touch of diarrhea. I'm going to bed, can we pick this up when I feel better? ... hopefully in the morning.

Well, it's two days later, and I don't know where the last forty-eight hours went. To be honest with you, I had to go back and reread the beginning of this chapter just to see what we were talking about. Talk about being knocked for a loop—I had no idea my body could have all the symptoms it did at one time.

So, why does God let bad things (like the flu) happen to good people (like me)? To continue to answer a question with a question—How else can it be done? It's not the best answer—an answer that's warm and fuzzy. But it's the truth, isn't it? Again, unless he decides to tell me right now why he allows certain things to happen, I really don't have a solid, concrete answer. But what if we try to figure it out together?

As we go down this particular journey, keep this question in the back of your head: "Does God *make* these things happen, or does God *allow* these things to happen?"

How many of us like being told what to do? How many of us would like being told we had to do anything (make that everything) someone else wanted us to, whenever that person felt like it? Yeah, my boss comes to mind, too! None of us would like to work for that person. Some of us have though, haven't we? You know, the boss who was the over-bearing, micro-managing, S.O.B. who no matter what you did, it was never enough. This is the guy/gal who on Monday said he/she (gotta watch out for the gender specific lawsuits) wanted it done this way, and then Tuesday rolled around and he/she wanted it done the exact opposite way. And then Wednesday came, and... You get the picture. We've all had that boss at one time or another. I remember the feeling in my stomach on the way to work,

can i get there from here?

just anticipating what lay in store for me. And once I got to work...no wonder we consume so many antacids!

What would our lives be like if we had to live with this boss? At least when he/she was only our boss, we knew we'd be done with him/her at the end of the day. What if this guy/gal—okay, this is getting ridiculous! I'm sticking with *him* and *guy* from now on. If you want to sue me because I am inferring that most jerk bosses are men, then go ahead—my address is at the end of the book. Your attorney(s) will need that to file the initial paperwork. This political correctness is getting out of hand!

So at the end of the day, you're done with *him*! On the way home from work you can finally unwind a little bit—only a little bit, because once you get home you have a whole bunch of other problems waiting for you. But at least you're away from this guy constantly telling you what to do.

Ah, home at last, you won't have to deal with him for another sixteen hours. Unless it's the weekend, and then you got two full days without worrying about making him happy. Time to kick your feet up and relax. Hey, if the chair from the first part of this book isn't ruined from the cat, go ahead and sit down on that and relax...

But wait—that same boss has followed you home. Now he's going to tell you what to do until tomorrow morning. He'll decide what you eat, what you wear, where you go, who you go there with, and on and on...

Important note—no joking here. If this is someone you're now in a relationship with, get help. Again, no joking, all kidding aside, if you are in a controlling relationship and this sounds like the person you're with—please seek counseling. I've been a cop too long to let this go by without mentioning it. These types of relationships often lead to violence (if it's not already there for you), and that violence is called Domestic Violence. Too many women (sorry guys—it's a fact) are abused and controlled in these kinds of relationships. Please, talk to someone who's trained in domestic abuse issues so you can learn about the cycle of violence and what you can do to reclaim control. Do whatever you have to do to be safe!

Everyone would have to agree that this kind of relationship is at the very least unhealthy, and more often than not—dangerous. We have all seen the dynamics in this kind of relationship. Maybe it was a co-worker, a relative, or a friend. Whoever it was, we were uncomfortable watching. We'd cringe at the way the abuser treated this person, and we couldn't understand why this person took the abuse.

We all want to have some freedom in our lives, don't we? Even the most over-protective parents let their children play unattended every now and then. What happens to those children who are raised by over-protective parents? We've all seen these kids, haven't we? We've rolled our eyes at their conduct; we've held our breaths with their tantrums; and we've bit our lip when we witnessed their unacceptable behavior. The over-protective parents never let their kids experience anything without supervision, without being told what they could and couldn't do. Over and over again, these kids were protected against anything that might harm them, even if their candy fell to the floor. No three-second rule for that kid!

Did those parents allow their children to experience anything in life? Did they allow their children to develop the social skills necessary to interact with other children? Did they make an excuse for their little darlings' behavior—because it could *never* be their fault? I get to see first-hand the results of parents who raise their kids in this fashion. Trust me, their teenage children have no concept of taking responsibility for anything, and they know mommy or daddy will get them out of whatever problem they find themselves in.

Question: Did you ever walk into the wrong public restroom? I just did—walked right into the ladies room at work. Ya think the lack of a urinal would've been a clue to me that I was in the wrong room? Or maybe the pink-colored tiles? Nope, I stood there like I was lost and didn't know where to turn. Anyone else ever been in that situation? Not the being in the wrong restroom part (although if you want to share your stories with me, I'd love to hear them); the part where you've been somewhere and couldn't figure out what was wrong. You didn't know why you were where you were (anyone confused by the *were*, *where*, *were* combo?); you didn't know how to get out of it, *and* you didn't know how you were gonna explain it. Sometimes life's like that, isn't it?

Sorry for the tangent; just another something I wanted to share with you.

As parents isn't it our job to prepare our children for the "real world"? One baby step at a time, we gently push and prod them toward independence. Think about it—we couldn't always hold the bottle for them, they had to learn to hold it on their own. Then came feeding themselves—food got everywhere in the beginning, didn't it? But eventually they learned where their mouth was and actually got more in their mouth than on their face. Next came dressing themselves, and so on and so on. Anyone other than me remember the first time you let your child cross the street without holding their hand? Scary, wasn't it? But that was the reward for teaching them—for encouraging them—to walk in the first place. Same with riding a bike, and driving a car.

By the way, if you've gotten through the driving part—God bless you! Six months of hell, as far as I'm concerned. For six months my sixteen-year-old son took the wheel with his learner's permit. At first, I couldn't understand why my right leg and ankle were so tired after driving with him. Then it hit me (ten bonus points if you got the "hit me" analogy with regards to a student driver). My leg and ankle were tired from hitting the imaginary brake pedal on the passenger side of the car!

But we made it, didn't we? Or should I say, they made it. Our reward was watching them grow. Watching them achieve more and more each day. Watching them become the *person* they are today. And if we were lucky we even got the chance to participate in some of the milestones they accomplished. No matter how mad or frustrated we get with them, we always seem to tell our friends how proud we are of them. And hey, nobody is suggesting that this journey comes without a price. Trips to the emergency room for stitches or casts; trips to their school to meet with the principal (courtesy of yours truly); trips to doctors' offices, and sometimes trips to rehab facilities. No one said this was going to be easy—raising a child. But we all go through it. Well, most of us.

If you're reading this and you've lost a child—my heart goes out to you. God bless you for what you've gone through and what you will continue to go through. No one can know what you're feeling; we can only offer our prayers and sympa-

can i get there from here?

thy. Hopefully, when you think of your child, you have enough memories of the good times that your face lights up.

Again, my heart goes out to you.

Even through the bad times, they were still our children, weren't they? We worked hard to get them where we thought they should be, and no fights along the way, right? If we could go back in time, can you remember how many times you gave your parents grief? Don't bother going for the calculator; we're all in the same boat. As kids, none of us wanted to be told what to do by our parents. They didn't know what they were talking about. We wanted our freedom and they wanted to keep us close to home. We fought for our independence and for our freedom from their control ever since we hit our teens.

Now for this, I have to tip my own hat; I'm an expert. Sorry, if there were ever credentials that permitted me to write this part of the book, they would be:

I'm a cop assigned to a high school, and I get paid to talk with teenagers all day long;

I've been a cop for more than 22 years, and have dealt with hundreds of teenagers and their parents;

I'm raising two teenage boys on my own;

I was a teenage boy!

Maybe you have similar credentials; at least all of us can say we were once teenagers. That in and of itself should give us some insight into the need teenagers have for independence and freedom. Our children are constantly trying to pull away, and we are constantly trying to reel them back in (ten points if you remember where this analogy was first used in this book). Sometimes I repeat myself—just like my father did ...

So, how do you think I'm going to tie this all together?

By now, you've figured out my method of madness, haven't you? Let's go back to the chapter—*"Are We God's Children?*." Too easy to see where I'm going? Well, we're gonna go down that road anyway. And why not, I got nothing else to fill this page—no more ideas have come to me, yet.

Are we God's children? Yep, we already answered that question. Does God know us? Yep again. Does God love us? He sure does. Could it be God's love that allows *everything* to happen to us? Because the way I see it, we can't have it both ways.

God knows and loves each and every one of us as his children. If we go back a few paragraphs we would all agree that as parents we have to give our children some freedom—we have to allow them to live. We do our best and then pray to God that they'll be okay. So as loving parents ourselves, we give our children the freedom—*the free will*—to live their lives. We don't tell them what to think, how to feel, and when to love. We would never think of those things in rearing our children. Discipline and control are two different things. So even though we never *want* to make that trip to the emergency room, or to the principal's office, or to the rehab center, we know that it could be a possibility. No matter how hard we try teach our kids right from wrong, eventually they're going to have to make their own decisions and sometimes those decisions get them in trouble. That doesn't mean we're bad parents; it doesn't mean we don't love them, and it certainly doesn't mean we *made* those things happen to our kids. Our decisions—*our love for them*—allow them to live. And sometimes life sucks and something bad happens.

How about that controlling S.O.B. boss we have? Or, remember when we were teenagers and wanted our freedom? Take either analogy (or both if you're an over-achiever like me) and follow this train of thought. Do we like being told what to do every second of the day we're at work? No, we want to scream and tell the jerk that we know what we're doing and to let us do our job. Imagine if that guy followed us to the break room or even into the bathroom. I can go anywhere with this...

He tells us in what order we should eat our lunch, down to counting how many times we chew each bite! And what about the bathroom? Even though I'm not a female-type, I know there are certain procedures you have to follow that us guys don't have to bother with. Can you imagine if your boss followed you into the bathroom and explained that procedure each and every time you had to go? Then he listened to your phone calls, read your e-mail, eavesdropped in the elevator, and then got in the car with you and told you how to drive home. And, of course, when you got home—well you get it. But this wasn't just for one day. No, this was every day of your life.

Even if this boss was the nicest guy in the world—the opposite of Mr. Jerk-O—he'd get on our nerves sooner than later. Anyone ever have that friend who wanted to be really helpful and who seemed to know everything? Their intentions were good, but God, could they test your limits! Nope, not even Miss Manners could stay by our side all day long and not irritate us. So we agree—we don't want to be controlled?

And what about the teenage years? Yeah, we knew what we were doing! Our parents didn't know a thing and we only wanted their advice when we asked for it. We only wanted their help when we needed it. We only wanted their love when it wouldn't embarrass us. Ah, to be a teenager—what an experience! But you know what? We all treated our parents like that, didn't we?

Maybe it was in our early teens, maybe in our mid teens, or maybe closer to adulthood, eventually our parents didn't have a choice. Sooner or later they handed us the keys; it was only a matter of time before our curfew got extended to midnight. Ultimately we won our independence. No matter when the transformation took place, we needed *our* parents to stop living *our* lives. Our parents had to stop telling us what to do, who we could hang-out with, and where we could go.

So whether we're teenagers or adults, we agree that we don't like being controlled. We don't want someone else to live their life through ours. We want our freedom—even freedom to make bad decisions. In other words, our will is our will. *Free will*. We're not puppets on anyone's string, and were not robots programmed to respond and react certain ways. Nope, instead we got another gift from God. And it's called free will.

Another reminder, and this is just my opinion. We're here trying to figure this one out together, and so far this is what we've got: We're God's children, and he knows and loves us. We don't want to be controlled or constantly be told what to do. We want free will.

So what does God do? He gives us free will. God is not the master puppeteer controlling our every move; he isn't the genius computer programmer; nor is he the ultimate ventriloquist putting words in our mouths.

I have got to admit something—I had no idea how to spell *ventriloquist*, I used spell check. Even though ventriloquist is hard to spell, it's still shorter than: *Guy who puts his hand up*

can i get there from here?

some dummy's rear end to move its mouth, and who speaks without moving his lips. I'll stick with using spell check. It's not easy though; Boomer (my retired black Lab) just jumped up on the couch next to me and put his head on the keyboard. Boomer is weighing in at a lean one hundred twelve pounds and his head is about the same size as the keyboard.

Wish me luck!

We were supposed to retire together, but he got arthritis in his legs; his thyroid gland is shot, and he's developed some fatty tumors on his hind quarters. He's not in pain; he just got lazy—and fat. So now that he's retired, he just lies around the house all day licking himself. And he can't wait to give me a kiss when I get home ... The things we do for love.

Back to the topic at hand. Since I started this chapter, the following things have happened:

A childhood friend was in a serious accident and now he's in the Trauma Intensive Care Unit (hang in there Dean- we're all praying for you); the mother of my fiancée's childhood friend died (I just got the phone call); one of my former students died; the priest who confirmed and married me, baptized my children, and presided over my parents' funerals died suddenly (thanks Father Moore, for everything), and my ex-wife is pissed at me and not speaking to me for sending her and her boyfriend flowers for Christmas. My fiancée and I thought it would be a nice gesture, you know, *peace on earth, good will toward men.* Well, that little act of kindness blew up in my face; she said I offended her by sending flowers. My mom used to say the road to hell is paved with good intentions ...

Some week, huh? I have no answers for any of these events. But I do remember what our police department chaplain once told me. His name is Reverend Jack. He's a former police sergeant from the same city where I was a paramedic, and he's helped a lot of police officers and firefighters in our county. Jack has a way of telling a story that relates to the problem at hand. He's truly a gifted preacher who can identify with what cops go through. He and I have had many theological discussions, and I consider him a friend as well as a confidant. During one of our discussions (usually on how crappy my life was going) Jack said the following: "This thing called life is tough; none of us are getting out of it alive!" Words of wisdom from a wise man. Thanks, Jack, for all you've given us.

Boomer's head is now on my thigh, and his left ear is covering the keys on the right side of the keyboard—and he's not budging! I'm gonna take a break and get some sleep. Whatta ya say we pick this up in the morning—when I can sit at the kitchen table without an over-affectionate Labrador Retriever on my lap. See you in the morning . . . God willing.

It's morning—I made it! Have you ever awakened with that sense of joy? You know, a love for life. The way I look at it, when my feet hit the floor in the morning—it's Thanksgiving. Everything else throughout the day is icing on the cake. Another way to look at it: When you wake-up this side of dirt—it's a good day.

Cliché's, aren't they great? Kinda like: "Why did God let this happen?" Perhaps it's because he loves us enough to allow us to live our lives. Good and bad. How else can he do it? I don't think we can pick and choose what times we want God

can i get there from here?

to intervene in our lives. Because—let's be honest—they would only be the times that we were getting ourselves in trouble, or the times we're about to experience something bad.

Would that really be a loving God? Remember the spoiled little brat? The one whose parents were so overprotective we wanted to smack both the kid *and* the parents silly? What kind of parents would they be? We've addressed this question earlier, but it bears repeating. What kind of parents would they be? Loving? Absolutely.

But what about:

Realistic? Is it realistic to believe a child can grow and flourish in that type of environment? A child who has no responsibility for his actions? A child who doesn't know how to deal with failure and disappointment?

Sensible? What kind of sense do these parents have? Don't they know what they are ultimately doing to their child? Do they know what type of child they are going to produce?

Caring? How much do these parents really care? If they really cared, wouldn't they help their children through the bad times instead of never allowing them to experience what life has to offer? And how much is this child going to care if everything was given to him, or if they were protected from the bad things in life?

Understanding? Do these parents really understand what it takes to raise a child? Do these parents really think that never letting their child fail at anything is going to help? Do these parents understand what will happen if they intervene in every fight and every disagreement, and in every conflict and every problem?

No one would argue that these parents love their kids,

but what kind of parents would they be? Since we already know we're God's children, doesn't that make him the definitive parent? So, if we follow this train of thought (told you it wouldn't be that hard), what kind of parent would God be if he intervened at every turn? It sounded so easy in the beginning, didn't it? If he's a loving God, then all he has to do is make sure these bad things don't happen to good people. But what's the criteria for *Bad Things* and *Good People*?

Bad Things. Are they physical things like accidents, illnesses, and diseases? Are they emotional things like heartache, sorrow, and anxiety? Are they financial things like bankruptcy, unemployment, and bad investment decisions? Are they material things like having your car stolen or losing your house to a fire? Are they the intangibles like the pro football player dropping the would-be go ahead touchdown pass? Or maybe your child striking out with the bases loaded? Perhaps dropping your keys into the Delaware River (my story for another time)?

Good People. Are they the ones who believe in God? Are they the ones who believe in God *and* go to church? Are they the ones who believe in God and go to church *more than twice a year*? Are they the ones who give to the charities? Are they the ones who give *a certain amount* to charities? Are they the ones who give a certain amount to *certain charities* (you know, God's favorite charities)? Are they the ones who go out of their way to help other people? Are they the ones who volunteer their time? Are they the ones who take in stray and wounded animals?

What criteria are we going to be satisfied with? Hey, I know he can do a lot of things, but I don't know if even God could come up with categories and sub-categories for *our* criteria. Now the simple question isn't so simple. God's perfection is God's perfection. We may not always understand it, but life is God's perfection.

Yeah right, you say. How can it be perfect with so many tragedies? I don't have that answer. Only God has that answer. But I do have a theory. Wanna hear it? I don't think these things are "God's will." By that, I mean I don't believe God *makes* these things happen. Rather, he *allows* them to happen. Just like he allows joy and happiness. God doesn't cause our happiness and joy, and he doesn't cause our hardships. I don't believe they are a test or a penance to pay here on earth. God has given us the freedom to live our lives. And he also gave that same freedom to the idiots who have killed others in drunk driving accidents, in horrible crimes of passion, and in other events that make us wonder. When a baby is killed in an accident, no one thinks the baby somehow deserved to die. But the freedom that God gave *everyone* may have contributed to the incident (and usually does).

I can't think of any other way to have it. If we didn't have freedom—radical freedom—what would our lives be like? Probably like some bad horror flick where some whacked-out dude uses mind control to gain power over the world. I wouldn't have the desire to write this book (unless it was God's will) and you wouldn't have the desire to read it (unless it was God's will). And if I couldn't write this, then you couldn't buy it. My children's college fund is riding on free will, can you believe that? And speaking of free will: where do some of these stores get the freedom to charge what they do for batteries? I think around this time of the year (Christmas) the battery companies get together with the toy companies, and the executives decide on a joint vacation for all their families! Just a hunch, I'm gonna look into this one a little further.

We still want it both ways, to a certain extent. Doesn't that sound just like us though? Hey, before we go further, are you starting to wonder why this chapter is so long? Me too! I guess it's probably because terrible things happen to us and our loved ones, and those things really test our faith more than anything else. I mean, think about it: You walk into a casino with one dollar in your pocket; you put that dollar in the first progressive slot machine you see; you pull the lever and win the jackpot of 3.6 million dollars! Is that the time you're going to look up at the sky and ask: "Why did you do this to me?!"

I didn't think so. It's not the good times that test our faith. It's the less-than-good times that leave us doubting his love for us. It's not the highlights of our lives that have us questioning his plan for us. It's the lowest points that leave us searching for answers. Here's something I've found myself doing for as long as I can remember: I only talk to God when I need something.

That's pretty poor, don't you agree? I can't remember the last time I gave thanks to God for something marvelous that happened, for something so magnificent I couldn't believe it. Now, if it was a close call and I came out of it alive, then yeah, I'm the first one to thank him. But what about the good things that happen to us? Am I the only one who is quick to blame (Him) when something goes wrong, but slow to praise (Him) when things go right?

Looking at it another way. We're all God's children and he's our parent. Imagine having kids like us! The only time our children talk to us is when they want something. Our children forget all about us until they're in trouble, and then the frantic call comes in. And then we're expected to be there immediately—just drop what we're doing because their little emergency is more important than anyone else's. When things go wrong in our children's lives because of poor planning, bad advice, or just plain stupidity—they blame us. And the jealousy! They're never happy with what they have; our children always want more. They get mad at us because their brother or sister has something bigger or brighter than their own. And on the few occasions they do talk to us as parents, with love and appreciation, it's usually just before they close their eyes in bed, too exhausted to express the full meaning of what they were trying to convey. Just a little bit of time for us at the end of their day.

How many adjectives can we come up with to describe these wonderful, beautiful, joyful, precious, caring, respectful, considerate children we have raised? Just a thought...

Before we call it another night: My oldest son has learned to do the laundry and it's a big help. Three men living together under one roof can get pretty ripe.... Don't get me wrong, I absolutely love having my boys with me. What a learning experience! And with learning comes ideas. Here's one: When you do the laundry, please fold it and put it away. Today, I came home to find that he did the laundry but was apparently too busy to fold it. So he dumped it on the couch in the living room. The same cozy couch I've been sitting on, with Boomer, as I type most of this book.

Well, Boomer now has decided to make himself comfortable on the pile of towels, shirts, and underwear that was dumped on the couch. Now for another idea: Find another spot for your retired bomb dog to sleep! The hair from his coat is everywhere this time of year, and now the laundry is covered in black fur. No towels for tomorrow's showers, so I gotta go put these back in. I should get to bed around midnight. Talk to you tomorrow.

Clean towels *and* clean sheets—what a life! How about summarizing this part so we can move on:

- We all agree we want our freedom, and we need it in order to grow.
- God wouldn't be the loving "parent" he is to all of us if he didn't give us our freedom.
- God does not cause the bad things in our lives, but he does allow them.
- Even the most beloved woman of the last 100 years was tormented by doubt because of the emotional pain and anguish she was suffering.

With all that in mind, can we make a quantum leap and assume that if God is a loving God, and if we are his children, then he would never wish harm to any of us? And we can go even further: he has been there, and will continue to be there for us through our worst tragedies and deepest sorrows. In fact, I believe God suffers right along with us—as any parent would do when his child is in pain. He suffers as though you are an only child—his only child. He feels your grief and he wants to comfort you.

And isn't that what we all want? God's comfort and God's

support. If all he provided was protection, how would we ever grow? How would we ever learn? If all God offered was protection, would we really have free will? In his book, *Credo*, William Sloane Coffin proposes that we have a God who provides us with minimum protection and maximum support. Does that make sense? Does it sound like what we've been talking about so far? None of us may like it, because when we experience pain, tragedy, loss, or suffering, the minimum protection from God doesn't feel like it's enough.

But it can be, if we are aware that he suffers right along with us. He feels our sorrow, our pain, and our anguish. He has to—how could we have these feelings if God didn't first have them? And joy, love, happiness—he has them too. Maybe we just don't think about those good feelings because when we're feeling them everything is going great in our lives. Imagine that; God feels our emotions—right along with us.

There's a verse in the Bible that bears this out. It also happens to be the shortest verse in the bible: When Jesus' friend Lazarus died, Jesus wasn't around to say goodbye. When he arrived a few days later, Jesus went to Lazarus' body. He was upset that he wasn't there to help his friend and he saw the sorrow in the faces of Lazarus' friends. Here's part of what is said about that reunion in John, Chapter 11, Verse 35: "*Jesus Wept.*"

Jesus knew what it was like to lose somebody; to feel grief and sorrow. Just like you and me, Jesus was heartbroken. And if Jesus was heartbroken, then God himself has felt heartbreak. God could have sent a robot to earth to teach us about what he wanted. Instead God sent his Son, Jesus, to us in the form of man. A man that had the same feelings as the people he was with. That's at least comforting, don't ya think? And

I think that goes to show that God will support us and comfort us—especially in our darkest hour.

But still, we expect God to protect us. After all, we're just human and we'd be crazy not to hope for his protection when bad things happen. But what would happen if all we looked for was God's protection? When we didn't get it would we become angry and bitter; maybe say some nasty things to him that we'll regret the rest of our lives? Maybe even tell him we don't want or need him anymore? When we do these things and take these actions aren't we missing the God who offers his support and comfort?

There was one time in particular in my life that I would have rather had God's protection than his comfort and support. For the guys out there, you should be able to identify with the pain I felt. You remember what kind of luck I have, and by now you've got a pretty good picture of my decision-making abilities as an adolescent. So what could possibly go wrong with me—as an adult—operating a motor boat capable of doing about forty-five miles per hour?

Here's the short story:

- Me, a co-worker (fellow cop), and my father-in-law on the Delaware River with an inflatable tube being pulled behind the boat.
- Pay-back time for what I did to my co-worker during his ride on the tube—A Coast Guard buoy tender was involved, and that particular boat creates a wake of about six feet.
- I'm on the tube hanging on for dear life watching my father-in-law and co-worker at the wheel laughing their asses off.

can i get there from here?

- We catch up to the buoy tender and I see the propeller come out of the water as our boat launches over the wake.
- I'm next—hanging onto an inflatable tube for dear life.
- The first bounce didn't hurt, and I don't remember the other bounces that were discussed later that evening.
- I do remember lying in the water pulling my bathing suit out of my butt, and I remember the pain.
- The impact of the water on my crotch as I completed a full summersault pushed what is meant to be hanging down up into a place where they aren't meant to be located.
- Grapefruit or softball sized—take your pick.
- Emergency room visit the following night to the same hospital where I worked as a paramedic.
- Jokes and Laughter from every nurse, paramedic, EMT and doctor who knew me … they actually called in paramedic units from other hospitals to take a look at the damage.
- Latex glove and KY Jelly to check *one last thing* (please tell me why?).
- Referral for a testicular ultrasound with a technician who lived in the same town that I worked—she said there was something about me that looked familiar.
- Note with a diagnosis of *Trauma and Contusion to Testicles* handed to shift sergeant who posted it on the bulletin board in the squad room.
- More jokes and laughter from my sympathetic brother and sister co-workers.
- Two weeks on light-duty wearing *loose* sweat pants.

In the category, "*Everything Happens for a Reason*," things actually worked out better than expected from this incident—something positive might have come out of it. Less than a year after the *accident* our son was born. We had been trying for a couple of years and nothing was working. This little incident put things on hold for a while—if you know what I mean...

After things had *completely* healed down there, we were able to try again at having a baby. And you know what? Nine months later out popped my first child. How about that! Now, I'm not saying that things got *knocked into* shape by the accident, but you have to wonder—could it have done something to get something going? Think about it, nothing was working for more than two years, then all of a sudden—*Splat*! My testicles are catapulted into my abdomen at forty-five miles per hour. A little rest and relaxation, and well, you can add your own adjective here...

So what would have happened if God protected me on that fateful day on the Delaware? Is it possible that something got jarred loose (jostled, bumped, tossed about—use whatever you want) that allowed me to have children? If that didn't take place, it's possible I still wouldn't have children. But that's not all: you would have never been able to read about this part of my life!

God was there; I was just in too much pain to see him. Maybe God's role isn't to stop all the bad things from happening but to be by our sides. Anyone remember the *Footprints* reference from earlier in the book? I believe, and I hope you would agree by now, that God really does carry us during the hardest times in our lives. Sometimes we look back and see only one set

can i get there from here?

of footprints because we want God's protection, but we fail to see his comfort and support. Well, that's just my opinion.

Is it possible God, at one time or another, has been *by our side leading us* in the right direction? Could it be that God has given us *what we need*? Can he *calm us* in a way that makes us feel *rested* and relaxed? Has our *faith* ever been *restored in him*? When we're *scared*, or in a *dark place*, can God make sure we *have no fears* because we know *he is with us*? Is God able to *comfort* us? Is it possible to think that everything will *turn out okay* because *he is with us* (and us with him) *forever*?

If you answered yes to any of these questions, congratulations! We all can probably answer *yes* to at least one of these questions. That means we're living proof of faith in a God who will be with us through our most troublesome times. We're living proof of something that was written thousands of years ago. Here's what someone far greater than me had to say about this living proof of faith.

> The 23rd Psalm:
> *The Lord is my Shepherd; I shall not want.*
> *He maketh me to lie down in green pastures; He leadeth me besides the still waters.*
> *He restoreth my soul; He leadeth me in the paths of righteousness for His name's sake.*
> *Yea though I walk through the valley of the shadow of death, I will fear no evil; for thou art with me; thy rod and thy staff they comfort me.*
> *Thou preparest a table before me in the presence of mine enemies; thou anointest my head with oil; my cup runneth over.*
> *Surely goodness and mercy shall follow me all the days of*

my life; and I will dwell in the house of the Lord forever.

Pretty cool stuff, don't you think? A poem—a psalm—written thousands of years ago that, to this day, offers comfort and promise for all of us. I left all the "eth's," "est's," and "thou's" in it, just the way it was written by David, because, I think, to try to modernize it would do it a disservice. It might be harder to read, but boy does it have magic when you do!

For me, one of the hardest obstacles (ten bonus points if you remember a better word for obstacle) I had to personally get past was accepting that, regardless of my goodness or faith, I can't escape the pain, tragedy, and suffering life *offers*. How about you? Have you been able to get this far in life without any struggles? Yeah, I know how ya feel!

God never promised us a life without pain, but I think we can be assured of his unconditional love, support, and comfort regardless of what predicament we find ourselves in. I'll end this summation with another passage from John, where Jesus tells his disciples, "In this world you have tribulation, but be of good cheer, I have overcome the world" (John16: 33, NKJV).

I think, I hope, we can all agree that because God is a loving God, he allows us to live our lives the way we want to. Sometimes it's not the way we would choose to live, but circumstances lead us to where we go. Free will has played a role and we are thankful for the opportunities that come with that freedom, yet because of that freedom, some pretty crappy things have happened to us and our loved ones. Bad things, at least in our eyes, have happened because God has allowed them to happen.

The good news: God knows what it's like to feel the

can i get there from here?

pain we've experienced. Because he knows what we're going through, God has a loving empathy that is unlike any other. None of us thinks we're more important than Jesus or that we deserve God's compassion more than his only Son. And I would bet that there aren't a whole lot of people that would want to compare themselves to Mother Theresa with respect to her caring, compassion, and sacrifice.

God didn't intervene in Christ's crucifixion. His only beloved Son, and God let him die on the cross. If Jesus didn't die that way, would we have salvation? I think we covered that earlier. So God must have known what he was doing in Calvary. And what about Mother Theresa? God must have had such a deep affection for her, and her work, that surely he could have made sure she didn't suffer the emotional turmoil we now know she had. Again, God must have known what he was doing—look at the wonderful work she accomplished in her life.

If God didn't intervene in his Son's death and if he didn't intervene in a great woman's emotional turmoil, what makes any of us think we're so great that he should stop the suffering in our lives? It's not because he doesn't care. He obviously cared about his only Son and he also cared about a magnificent woman who was doing his work here on earth. And it's not because he doesn't love us. God's love for his only Son, for Mother Theresa, and for all of us is so great it can't be measured.

God has been there, and will continue to be there, to comfort and support us in our darkest hours. In closing, God allows bad things to happen because he loves us enough to allow them to happen. Can an answer that simple be the real answer? God, I hope so...

But here's a question that I'll never be able to understand: Why do they use alcohol to sterilize the injection site on the arm of a condemned killer before they stick him with a needle to put him to death?

so, what are you looking for?

Most of the time I was looking for a place to run with an escape route. Whether it was running from the cops when we threw water balloons at cars on mischief night, running from the cops when we broke into a new house under construction, running from the cops when we cut school, running from the cops when we *borrowed* the neighbor's car, or running from the cops when we were drinking in the woods, we were always running—looking for a way out. And just about every time we made it out, we found a way to make it back to the house. Except the few times we weren't quick (or smart) enough.

Have you ever been in that predicament? No, not running from the cops as a juvenile delinquent (although, I'd love to share stories with you); I'm talking about running from something you've done in an effort to get away. Maybe you were running from a lie, or running from your past, or maybe even running from love. Whatever it was, we've all been there. For me, I just happened to be able to get a jump start (10 points for picturing me jumping over fences being chased by the cops) on running from things. At an early age I learned to search for escape routes. Now that I look back on my life, my instincts might have done me well in keeping from getting caught, but those same instincts also gave me reason (and justification) to find escape routes later in life that would not serve me so well. Escape routes were what I was looking for in so many aspects of my life. Ways to escape pain, heartache, suffering, sorrow, and anger. So many times these emotions were covered up with an escape route—I just ran away.

Sometimes that's all we're looking for—escape routes. We spend so much time running *from* something that we forget we can also run *toward* something. We actually have the same ability to run toward something good as we do to run away from something bad. And isn't it better to run toward something that can protect us, maybe even save us, than to run away from something, with nowhere in particular to go?

I kept running away from the people who were there to protect me—police officers, teachers, neighbors, and of course—my parents. I didn't know that I *could* stop running, much less learn *how* to stop running, until just recently. When you learn a skill at an early age, you tend to keep getting better at it until something comes along to change that skill. You don't have to be a kid to be so dumb or naïve to ignore advice or suggestions—signs along the way—that might give you reason to stop and take a look at what's going on around you. Why do we run from the ones who have our best interest at heart? I wish I had an answer that made sense, but all I can offer is an excuse: we're probably scared.

What are we really afraid of? Is it fear of failure, fear of rejection, fear of commitment, or fear of disappointment? Could it be a combination of some or all of these? How many more fears can you add to this list? Go ahead and take your time, I gotta go to the doctor for a check-up—who knows how long this is gonna take.

That didn't take too long. It was my annual visit to the "butt doctor" as my son calls him. And it wasn't as bad as I thought it would be—as bad as I *feared* it would be. I was lying there on my side with my pants down around my ankles and my knees bent, and I got to thinking. Yeah, I know—too easy; forget it, no points there! Butt I got to thinking (now you can give yourself the points for the but misspelling): Why was I afraid? I had a lot of fear and anxiety going into the doctor's office; yet when the visit was over, I realized it wasn't that bad. How many times in life has that happened? We go into something fearing the worst, and when it's over, we look back and think, "What was I so afraid of?"

If fear got the best of me and I didn't go to my appointment, I would have been left wondering if everything was okay. How about you? Have you ever not done something because of fear? And then thought, "What if?" or "If only..." I'd run out of paper if I counted all the times I didn't do something because of fear. And when we fail to do something we should do, we end up going in a different direction—a direction that we don't always know where we're heading. Then

can i get there from here?

we start to look for something else. And since that's the title of this chapter, what do you say we go down that road?

Hey I didn't know what my doctor was looking for, but I had faith he knew what he was doing. Any analogies come to mind? I have a lot of jokes that come to mind—all you have to do is give me a proctologist, and the punch-lines just jump into my head.

So, what are we looking for? If you could pick only three, which ones would they be?

Happiness	Security	Love	Strength
Prosperity	Respect	Health	Hope
Contentment	Devotion	Success	Pleasure

What if you could only pick one? Talk about prioritizing! Aren't you glad we don't have to narrow it down? We can have any and all of them—as well as the ones not on this list. So with all these choices, we can have it all, right? Or is it possible that we can look, and look, and look, and still not find what we're looking for? That was me for a long time. I was looking for something; I just couldn't narrow it down. At least that's what I thought. I thought I had to come up with something specific in order to find happiness—to find what it was that I was looking for. Was it the perfect marriage, the best job, the nicest house, or some good friends? Where could I find the right training, get the best experience, and obtain the proper credentials to be a good cop or paramedic? And what about: where do I go to be a good parent, to be a good friend, or to be a good brother and son?

I was looking everywhere for everything. And ya know

what I found out? By looking everywhere, for everything, I wound up missing everything, everywhere. Yep, when you're looking for everything, you end up finding nothing.

Think of life as a maze—in the dark—with no map— and no direction out. What would you look for? Do you start with a map? What about a light? How about a plan?

Wouldn't it be better to think of these things before you entered the maze? Think about it. Most explorers have an idea of what they're looking for *before* they go out looking, don't they? Most naturists have an idea of what they want to find *before* they grab their binoculars, don't they? And most gastrointestinal doctors have an idea of what they're looking for *before* they ... wait, I think he found the ex-wife's lawyer's watch. Sorry, I couldn't help myself! Aren't you glad I'm not bitter about the divorce? Actually I'm not—honest; we both did the best we could in a pretty crappy (huh?) situation.

So, what if we used the aforementioned (I always wanted to use that word) analogies (minus the doctor—unless you have a mind like me) and thought about what we're looking for before we head out? Someone once said: "If you don't stand for something, you'll fall for anything." And someone else once said: "A ship with no direction will be blown into any port when a storm comes." Maybe both were said by the same person, who knows? But the point is we all need some sort of plan, some sort of direction, if we want to find what we're looking for.

With a plan our search will be more effective. 1. How do we come up with a plan; 2. How do we get direction? Great questions! Who knows the answers? Come on, it's not that hard ... is it? Where would I go to find direction in life? Where would I look to find a plan for life?

"*Give me a B. Give me an I. Give me another B. Give me an L. Give me an E. What's that spell?*" "*BIBLE, BIBLE—Yeah, BIBLE!*"

I'm sorry, I couldn't help it (again). I thought you might be getting tired, so I threw in a cheer to get things going. You know, like a group of college cheerleaders at the big game.

It's the Apostles against the Pharisees in the championship game.

Announcer:

"*The apostles are led by their captain, Paul, who's had an incredible year. He's been playing great with help from a couple of big men up front. Matthew, Mark, Luke, and John have put up equally impressive numbers of late and they seem to have laid the foundation for the rest of the team…*"

Can't you picture the game? The cheerleaders would be calling out cheers from the sidelines.

"*Bring-Out-The-Sinners… Bomp-bomp, Bah-dah-dah*"

Or

"*We are good—We are fine—We're the followers of the Divine*"

Okay, not my best stuff, but you get the picture. Now, where the heck was I? I really hate it when this happens. I gotta scroll up and see where I was—wait a minute…

Bible, B-I-B-L-E, Bible. Now I got it. Why not look in the Bible for direction and a plan? It seems like that would be a great place to look. What's it say in "The Good Book," as my father used to call it, about direction and a plan for life?

The steps of the godly are directed by the Lord. He delights in every detail of their lives. Though they stumble, they will not fall, for the Lord holds them by the hand.

Psalm 37:23–24 (NLT)

Your word is a lamp to my feet and a light to my path.

Psalm 119:105 (NIV)

The way of man is not in himself; it is not in man who walks to direct his own steps.

Jeremiah 10:23 (NKJV)

But seek first his kingdom and his righteousness, and all these things will be given to you as well. Therefore do not worry about tomorrow, for tomorrow will worry about itself. Each day has enough trouble of its own.

Matthew 6:33–34 (NIV)

I'll stop with that last one from Matthew. God created each and every one of us for a purpose. Now ya gotta admit, that's pretty cool! If you want to search Google or Yahoo for some more passages, go ahead. I just put down the first couple I could find. Both the Old and New Testaments tell us to look toward God for direction. Can it really be that simple? I guess it's a matter of trust. *Should* we trust our Lord to lead the way? *Can* we trust our Lord to lead the way? There's a little story that I think makes that point. I found it on the web—www.promiseofgod.com.

It's called God and the Spider:

During World War II, a US Marine was separated from his unit on a Pacific island. The fighting had been intense, and in the smoke and the crossfire he had lost touch with his comrades.

Alone in the jungle, he could hear enemy soldiers coming in his direction. Scrambling for cover, he found his way up a high ridge to several small caves in the rock. Quickly he crawled inside one of the caves. Although safe for the moment, he realized that once the enemy soldiers looking for him swept up the ridge, they would quickly search all the caves and he would be killed.

As he waited, he prayed, "Lord, if it be your will, please protect me. Whatever your will though, I love you and trust you. Amen." After praying, he lay quietly listening to the enemy begin to draw close. He thought, "Well, I guess the Lord isn't going to help me out of this one." Then he saw a spider begin to build a web over the front of his cave.

As he watched, listening to the enemy searching for him all the while, the spider layered strand after strand of web across the opening of the cave. "Hah," he thought. "What I need is a brick wall and what the Lord has sent me is a spider web. God does have a sense of humor."

As the enemy drew closer he watched from the darkness of his hideout and could see them searching one cave after another. As they came to his, he got ready to make his last stand. To his amazement, however, after glancing in the direction of his cave, they moved on.

Suddenly, he realized that with the spider web

over the entrance, his cave looked as if no one had entered for quite a while. "Lord, forgive me," prayed the young man. "I had forgotten that in you a spider's web is stronger than a brick wall."

We all face times of great trouble. When we do, it is so easy to forget what God can work in our lives, sometimes in the most surprising ways. And remember with God, a mere spider's web becomes a brick wall of protection.

Author Unknown

Who'd-a-thunk it? A spider's web was more protective than a brick wall. Is the story real? Beats me. It'd be really awesome if it was. Regardless, the point remains the same. Sometimes ya just gotta have faith...

And if we injected a little bit of faith into our search, maybe it would be easier to find what we're looking for in the first place. If only we were able to replace fear with faith. Now that's an idea! All we need is a little motivation, right?

There are many great motivational speakers out there and some of them are even worth the price they charge. I found one in particular to be a man of both faith and integrity. His name is Dr. James Reese. He's a retired FBI agent and one of the agency's original "Mind Hunters." He travels the world speaking to companies and organizations—in addition to being an expert in stress and threat assessments—as well as a best-selling author. I had the opportunity to meet Dr. Reese while I was a chairman for a training conference. Dr. Reese literally captivates an audience with his wit and anecdotes. Here's one thing he said that I will always remember:

"You've got to want it more than you fear it."

Sounds simple, doesn't it? Just *want* it more than you *fear* it. I thought so until I started to take inventory of my life. The question just kept coming at me: did I want to have something more than I was afraid of having it? I can replace the word *something* in the previous sentence with a lot of things that I either didn't finish or never started because of fear. How about you? Looking back, have you ever passed-up something, given-up on something, or lost interest in something because you were more afraid of it than your desire to have it? Did *fear* replace *faith*? Ask me that same question, and we'd be here all day discussing my projects that I never finished. So we gotta flip things around: replace fear with faith. Okay, how are we gonna do that?

Beats me. I'm just a cop trying to find my way through this thing called life just like you ...

All right, ya paid for the book and are probably expecting some kind of answer. Or ya borrowed the book and wanna get through it so you can give it back to the person you borrowed it from (another sentence ending in a preposition— good thing we're almost finished). Hey, are you like me? Do you try to figure out how much longer you have to go before you finish a book? I try to figure out what percent or fraction of the book I have to go before I can put it down for good. I estimate that by comparing the number of pages (the thickness) I've read with the number of pages (hopefully less thickness) I have to go. If you're like me, stop now and take a look. We're almost done (probably should've used *finished*)! Now, let's get back to this so we can both take a break ...

We'll get through the remainder of the book together; I promise. Let's work this out *collectively* (I wanted to use *together* again, but since I used it in the previous sentence I had to find a synonym instead). One last question: What's a synonym for Thesaurus, and where would you find it?

First, I think we have to accept ourselves and be happy. Sounds simple enough. So let's just do it—we'll be happy. We'll be happy with our life—with what God has given us. We'll stop complaining, accept ourselves, and accept others.

Come on, we're in this together, remember? If I can do it, so can you! Have you ever known someone who's a professional complainer? Yep, me too. And I betcha they're not the same person. There are a whole bunch of them out there just waiting to be heard. Go ahead and listen to them if you want, but I think I'd rather spend my time sticking my hand in a blender.

It's amazing how much happiness can be sucked out of us just by listening to other people. First we try to be nice by listening, and before you know it, we're just as miserable as they are. Take the following analogy anyway you want and see if it fits some of the *happiness vacuumers* you know.

If you take a job as a proctologist, don't sit around and complain that you have to deal with assholes all day.

I've been waiting to use that line since the second chapter. Boy does it feel good to finally get it out…

How about another analogy that might not only make more sense, but also be a little more topical to what we're looking for. It's the album analogy. For those of you who are too young to remember that music was once played from vinyl—think of a *really big* CD. For those of us who remember what it was like to listen through the static and skips to get to our favorite drum solo—welcome home! Can you believe we actually had to get up from the sofa and lift the needle off the record if we didn't want to hear the next song? No remote control for us, we got up and changed the tracks *ourselves*! Could it be that remote controls are just as much to blame for our obesity problem as *Dorito's Cool Ranch* chips? I could eat a bag of them in one sitting, but at least I got some exercise as I listened to my albums.

Here's the point: We went out and bought our albums because we either liked the group or our friends had them and we wanted to be cool—like them. Either way, we bought the *whole* album. We bought the albums, took them home and played them. Sometimes we played them so much they wore-out, and we had to put a penny on the arm of the record player to keep the needle from skipping. Remember that? Ah, the good ole days...

Life—our life—is like an album, or a CD (but it's a really big CD). We can't just listen to the tracks we like; we have to accept the *entire* album—even the songs that we're not that fond of. Back then (God, I sound like my father) we listened to the whole album, sometimes just to get to the last song, if that was a favorite. Now, with CD's, we can just use the remote to skip past the songs we don't like to get the one or two that we do like.

Man, how things have changed. Have our lives changed with the times? Are we a people that now fast-forward to the parts of our lives that we like, while at the same time skipping past the parts we don't like? Is that what it's come to? Has technology really done this to us? God, I hope not. But it's a scary thought, ya gotta admit.

What do you say we look at our lives as if they *are* that album we had in high school? You know, that favorite album we could never get rid of—even if we had to weigh the needle down with a stack of pennies. We accepted all of it back then, didn't we? We thought the album cover had the best artwork or coolest pictures, and we listened to it in our bedrooms all night long. Not only did we memorize our favorite songs, we also knew the words to the rest of the songs on the album that came blaring out of those huge speakers in the corners of the room. That album became our favorite either *because of* all the songs on it or *in spite of* all the songs on it. Either way it was our album and we loved it—we accepted it. Can't we take a chance and look at life the same way?

What if we saw other people as albums? Sure they have some scratches in them and there are a few songs that get on our nerves (or under our skin), but all-in-all the record is okay. Come to think of it, other people's songs are pretty nice—we might even have the lyrics memorized! Maybe that album is a co-worker, a friend or neighbor, a family member, or perhaps a boss, all interesting records in album covers otherwise known as skin. Each has a certain beauty all their own. After all, some of our favorite albums had covers that might not have been all that pretty, but the songs were just amazing. I guess mom was right: *It's what's on the inside that counts.*

So how about getting over this hurdle together—the hurdle of accepting ourselves and being happy. Let's just look at ourselves, and each other, as albums. We may not like every song, but for the most part, we like the album and we're happy with it. I bet it's gonna be harder to accept our own album than to accept the albums of others. Why is it that we're harder on ourselves than we are on others? We

can i get there from here?

gotta move on—so let's agree to accept and be happy with who, what, why, and where we are. Okay?

You know where I found some of my favorite albums? At the mall. The mall also had *Spencer's Gifts* and *A Shop Called East*, but that's another story for another book. The mall record stores had all the albums (the album *covers*) I wanted on display, and all the cool kids hung-out there. Once we were done checking everything out at the record store, we spent the rest of our time hanging out and getting in trouble. The mall has so many memories for me as kid growing up. Some of my memories had good outcomes, while others—well not so good. But all of them ended with fun—and more often than not, a chase out into the parking lot by mall security.

Teenagers at the mall, Scenario number one:

Stand under the open stairs at either end of the mall and look up the girl's (sometimes grown women's—if we were lucky) skirts.

Teenagers at the mall, Scenario number two:

Stand on the second floor balcony and look down the girl's blouses—hoping for an older woman to walk by.

Teenagers at the mall, Scenario number three:

This one's my favorite, I have to admit: Go to Woolworth's and buy as much Mr. Bubbles as you and your friends can afford; sit on the ledge of the water fountain (the really big one at the end of the mall); casually, behind your back, pour the contents of Mr. Bubbles into the fountain; nonchalantly walk away as if nothing happened. Then watch the magic. That end of the mall was shut down for hours while they cleaned-up the mess.

Thank God there were no video surveillance cameras back then!

I told you the memories always ended in fun. I still like to go to the mall and walk around—just to *people watch*. Only now I don't stand under the stairs or at the balcony—a cop can get a bad reputation doing those things. But you know what's funny? I still see kids doing what I was doing way back then. And they try to look so innocent. I just look at them and smile (I should give them some pointers)—what memories ...

I have to thank our pastor Andrew for inspiring the following:

Now I go into stores and look around—*just looking*. That's what I tell the ever-helpful sales person who approaches me.

"Can I help you?" "Is there something I can help you with?"

"No thanks, I'm *just looking*."

I go from store to store meandering in and out while my fiancée does her shopping. One time she talked me into going into a ladies clothing store to shop with her. Well, it only took about two minutes for me to get bored, so I walked off on my own while she held up and inspected every sweater on the rack. A nice sales person came up to me and asked if I needed help. Before I could stop it, "No thanks, I'm just looking," came out of my mouth. And I'm wearing a Fraternal Order of Police t-shirt with a big logo on the front. Great, a perverted cop snooping around a women's clothing store—*just looking*. I couldn't get out of there fast enough. As if that wasn't humiliating enough, I sat on a bench outside the doors of the store. I thought I was safe. I was out of the store, sitting on a bench like all the other guys whose significant others were enjoying their shopping experience.

can i get there from here?

All was good until the cute little sales person—the one who asked me if I needed any help—came out of the store on her break. And who's the first person she makes eye contact with? The perverted cop—the one just looking—who just left her store. She sees me sitting outside the store as if I'm stalking everyone who comes out or goes into the store. She saw me, and she walked away with a look of disgust on her face. Sometimes you just can't catch a break.

That's still not as embarrassing as sniffing around (thanks to Larry The Cable Guy) Victoria's Secret telling the sales girl I was *just looking*... for a gift for my mom. Time to move forward—I've had three cups of coffee this morning and stuff is starting to happen. There are noises coming from my stomach that I haven't heard before.

The mall and life—what a comparison. Here's the way I see it. We go into the mall looking; looking for something that will jump out at us. Very few of us have a defined objective when we arrive. We're just there to walk around and look. Hey, maybe I could get some exercise in the sneakers I bought in the shoe store while showing-off my hot body (get in line, ladies) wearing the sweat suit I bought in the sporting goods store, and at the same time checking out my new watch (get it:... *at the same time* and *watch*—ah, forget it).

But with no idea of what we're looking for, what do we end up doing? For me, it's either buying something I don't need (sneakers, sweat suit, and watch) or filling-up on some calorie and fat laden junk from the food court. I go there with good intentions, but end up walking out either holding a bag full of something that I don't need or a stomach full of something I shouldn't have (insert another donut or similar joke of your own choosing here...). And all I did was go there to walk around, or to look around, or to kill some time. Ahh, the best intentions...

How does that compare to my life? When I think of the times I went somewhere—emotionally or spiritually, perhaps—I don't remember having a plan of where I wanted to go. I walked around life for a long time, *just looking*. Life can be a lot like a mall: There are a lot of stores with a lot of variety. It seems like there's something for everyone. Some of the stores' advertising persuades us to go in and look around. We're able to walk by others without a second glance. And every store has someone there who wants to help us.

Is there someone in your life who's there to help you? Maybe a friend or colleague, it could be a relative or a guy at one of those meetings. How many times do we push these people away? We go in and out of their stores (their lives), just looking. They want to help us or offer us something, and we politely turn them down. Maybe it's the color of their album cover, perhaps we've heard a few of their songs and we weren't impressed, or sometimes it's just that the songs on the album aren't up to our caliber.

We have no problem going into their stores to look around—just don't get too close and make us feel uncomfortable. Think of all the people we push away and what we might have lost by doing so. During any given day we have more opportunities than *just looking*; we have opportunities to really make a difference.

"Hi, how ya doing?"

"Here, let me get the door for you."

"Please, take this seat I'm waiting for a friend."

It doesn't take much, does it? A few kind words, even a simple smile, can make someone's day. And by making someone's day, we've just helped ourselves. We'll get back to that in a minute. But there's a point that has to be brought out before I forget (it's 12:44 a.m. and I don't know if I'll remember later). What if, "*Can I help you*," didn't come from the sales person? What if the voice was a little deeper, had a little more oomph to it? Yeah—him! He's there, waiting for you to come into the store. When you do and you're asked, "*Can I help you?*" do yourself a favor and swallow your pride. Give thanks that God is there for you and his door is always open.

So many times we pretend we don't need his help, his direction, or his guidance and we tend to try it alone. In this *Mall of Life*, there's a store called *J.C. and His Salvation*. Next time you get a chance, stop in and look around. But remember, when you're asked, "Can I help you?" bite your tongue before, "No thanks, I'm just looking," comes out. Give it a thought ... or two.

Back to helping ourselves by making someone else's day. Have you ever heard of Serotonin? It's a chemical in our brains that regulates our moods. Basically, the more Serotonin we produce, the happier we are. Most, if not all, anti-depressant drugs either *stimulate* the release of Serotonin or *simulate* it in the brain to make the body believe Serotonin has been released into the bloodstream. There have been numerous studies on the effects of Serotonin, and new x-ray technology actually allows doctors and scientists to see its effects on the brain.

One study that was recently conducted astounded a lot of people in the scientific and psychological communities. The study found that when someone was *the victim* of a random act of kindness—let's say a door was held, a nice comment was made, or something was picked up that they dropped—that victim's Serotonin level went up. That's not that surprising, after all, who doesn't appreciate a kind act. The study went on to find that the *doer* of the random act of kindness also had his level of Serotonin go up. And here's the really interesting part—*witnesses* of the random act of kindness had their Serotonin levels go up as well. Can you believe that? Just watching a kind act can make your brain release the same chemical that's used in antidepressant medication. Imagine what we could accomplish if we just committed one act of kindness each day. A nation of medicated people could actually lose its dependence on at least one type of medicine by doing something good for someone else. Now there's a plan I can live with!

Maybe I'm being a little too optimistic, although when you think about it, anything's possible. But, we're still skeptical, aren't we? We're still not sure it can be that simple. Come on, you're saying, all those self-help books talk about searching for the perfect... Or searching for the ultimate... And here's my favorite, "Looking out for Number One." All those books, all that medicine, and all those one-hour sessions with our counselors. How much money do you think we spend on trying to find what we're looking for? Just turn on the TV and before too long you'll find an infomercial or a talk show or some other kind of program designed specifically to tell you what you're doing wrong with your life and how this or that can make you better.

Can finding what we're looking for be as simple as looking in the right direction? Nobody wants to put anyone out of business, and if a person really needs counseling, then by all means they should seek a professional. God knows I spent enough time with one going through the divorce. And if anxiety is wreaking havoc in someone's life, antidepressants can have a significant impact in getting that person back on track.

But what about the long haul? Are we really supposed to be dependent on psychologists and counselors for the rest of our lives? Are we really supposed to be taking "happy pills" until we no longer know what we're doing? If you were to read the ads in some of the magazines, or watch enough TV, you'd think that's what we're supposed to do. Some of the major drug companies have a ton of money invested in their products, and their marketing and sales forces seem to have most of the medical profession believing *their* pills are necessary for *our* health. Nothing self-serving in their propaganda, right?

Medication and therapy are good for the acute phase of our problem. That is, the initial incident, and the time after it, that has caused the symptoms and problems we face. Does the *ethical* doctor really want you returning once a week for the rest of your life? Does the *ethical* pharmaceutical company want you on their drug for the rest of your life? If driven by ethics, then I believe the answer to both questions is *no*. If driven by greed and ego, the answer is a resounding *yes*. The ethical folks would like you and me to be weaned-off their product or services so that we can deal with life on our own. Their hope *should be* that their product or service has taught us or helped us deal with our problems until we are strong enough to handle them on our own.

So who do we trust? Who can we trust? Where do we start? In times of need, the phone book is nothing more than a laundry list of professionals listed alphabetically. How do we know which one will be the best for us; which one will keep our needs first?

I've been there, it ain't easy.

Marriage counseling—about a hundred-or-so listed;

Post Traumatic Stress Disorder—a couple dozen, give or take a few;

Adolescent Issues—another two or three dozen;

Anger—a handful

What about all the initials after their names: PHD, MD, LCSW, DO, LPN, RN, and on and on and on. Who's better, an MD or a DO? Who's best for what I need, a PHD or LCSW? What about my kids, who will be the right choice for them? And so, the search continues—looking for the right person. Sometimes friends or family members will refer you to the right professional. Most times, at best, it's a hit-or-miss proposition.

If only I could turn to someone who will:

- Have my best interests at heart
- Honestly get to know me in order to offer me the best treatment
- Be selfless in his approach rather than selfish
- Offer what's best for me instead of being self-serving
- Have the most experience in the profession
- Have the best success rate in the business
- Have a product from which I will never need to be weaned
- Will keep me as his patient for the rest of my life, free of charge

Hmm, who could that be? Ponder that while I go check my caller ID. The phone's been ringing for a while, but I didn't want to stop and answer it. I'll be right back after I see who's been trying to call me.

I'm back. Sorry it took so long; I figured I might as well get a cup of coffee while I was up. Now it's just me, you, Boomer and a hot cup of coffee (two sugars and a little cream). The caller ID showed a couple of out-of-area numbers. I'm glad I didn't jump up and run to answer those solicitation requests. Doesn't that just piss you off? They call either during dinner or before bed; as if we have nothing better to do than take their calls. That's why caller ID is so great! It allows you to screen your calls before you pick-up the phone. If I had nothing better to do, I would have checked the caller ID to see who was calling. But since I've got this book to finish, I just stayed put and kept on typing. No need to thank me. You couldn't read any faster than I was typing anyway. Come to think of it, it really wouldn't have mattered if I stopped typing and answered the phone, would it? You still would be right here reading this sentence regardless if I stopped and answered the phone. So I let it ring for nothing?

Have you ever done that? Ever let the phone ring because you were too busy doing something else to answer it? I'm just like you; I figure if it's important they'll leave a message, and if they don't leave a message I can always check the caller ID. Modern technology to the rescue.

And if you're like me, I bet there's been more than one call that you wish you did answer—the message that was left was an emergency. The five minutes it took for us to play the message really hurt us by not getting important information in a timely manner. Or maybe the person calling was in such a panic that they hung-up before our out-going message to them even finished. Life can be like that; ya never know who's calling.

Wanna know who keeps calling, hoping against hope that we answer the phone? The caller ID won't show his number, but his message has been left for more than two-thousand years. Yep, right again! God, Jesus, Lord, Yahweh, The One, I Am—he's used all those names and his solicitation is a 24/7 proposition.

He keeps calling. When are we gonna answer his call? It's not like we owe him anything, right? Why should we take time out of our busy day to take his call? Come on, if it's really important he'll leave a message. He keeps calling anyway, so I'll answer it when I have more time and when I'm not so busy.

Telemarketers are a real *pain in the ass* (my dad abbreviated it to PITA). But what if it's not a PITA solicitation? What if it's him?

Maybe that call provides the answer to what we're looking for. Perhaps his offer will provide the answers we need to keep from running. His voice will offer comfort and direction. The book he's pushing offers acceptance *and* answers *and* comfort *and* direction. His doors are always open and he promises you'll find what you're looking for inside. He offers lifetime treatment options with an eternal guarantee

I guess it comes down to trust ... and faith. We all have a desire to explore—to search and look around. It's been with us for as long as we can remember. Our parents could barely keep track of us when we were toddlers; as soon as they took their eyes off us we were gone. When we got older, we longed to set out on our own. Even if it was just a hike in the woods, we wanted to do some exploring ourselves. Sometimes we got lost—and scared. Especially if it started to get dark!

I remember being lost in the woods by our house. I was about ten or eleven and got all turned around on a hike. It was around Thanksgiving and the sun was setting before dinnertime. I was scared, cold, and alone. Every noise made me jump. The shadows of the trees were turning to darkness and my heart was pumping. I didn't tell my parents where I was going because I had been in those woods my entire life. My brother and I played all sorts of games and built a whole lot of forts in those woods, so I thought I knew every inch. Apparently I was wrong.

First I heard his voice—he was calling my name. Then I saw the light coming toward me—getting brighter and brighter as his voice got louder. When the light hit me I knew I was going to be okay. My dad had found me. When I didn't make it home for dinner, dad reassured mom and my brother, and then set off to find me. And dad was smart enough to make sure he had batteries in his flashlight. Funny how fathers just seem to know what to bring...

My dad said he knew what I liked to do and he remembered talking to me about exploring in the woods. With that information he was able to get a general idea of where I was probably hiking. Even though he had never been with me in that part of the woods, my father knew where to find me. My father made sure I was found—he knew where to find me. That was amazing. But he didn't just find me. He led me out of the woods (out of the darkness) and he walked me home. He was going to make sure I made it home.

Fathers are like that. It's one thing to find us, but every dad out there wants to make sure we make it home.

Once I got home and got warm, dinner was served. My mom held dinner and made sure it was still hot for my dad and me. We all sat down as a family to eat—together.

Anyone wanna make a comparison with this story to something bigger? Go ahead, I teed it up for ya—give it a nice hit and see how far you can drive it. I'm sure you can take this and...

Hold on, my phone's ringing.

anything else?

Yeah, there are a few things left. Like how did I get this far in the book? I never thought I would be able to accomplish something like this. Have you ever felt that way? Have you ever had so much doubt in yourself that you purposely stopped yourself from going after a dream? Me too!

But, has someone ever had so much faith in you that they knew you "could do it"? That's where I find myself these days. Think about it for a minute; how many people in our lives have had faith in us? How about taking a minute to write down a short list of the names of those people who have come into our lives, for however brief a period of time, and had faith in us. My list would start with my parents, my brother, and my children. They're the easy ones. What if we think deeper and spend a little more time on this? Take your time; my son's home sick from school today and I'm going to go check in on him. I'll be back.

Wow, quite a list, don't ya think? My list included my teachers—which by now you know I have an affinity for. I thought about all that they have given me. Not just the readin,' writin,' and 'rithmatic, but also what they taught me about life. They refused to give up on me; they had faith in me. What a gift to give a kid who didn't give a damn about himself!

My list continues with my paramedic training. At the time I was accepted into the program, I was only eighteen years old. The director of the program was taking a chance on me. No one my age had ever been accepted into this type of program before. The medical director had faith that I could do it; he had faith in my skills and knowledge of emergency medicine. With the reputation of the entire program on the line, someone had enough faith in me to take a chance—what a gift!

Another person who had faith in me was my flight instructor. But not any old flight instructor. I always wanted to learn how to fly, so I took an introductory lesson about four years ago. I didn't want to fly airplanes; nope, I wanted to learn how to fly helicopters. Helicopters have been described as machines with a thousand moving parts that have no logical reason to fly. If learning to fly an airplane is like learning to ride a bike, then learning to fly a helicopter is like learning to ride a unicycle—balanced on top of a beach ball.

Here's what Harry Reasoner had to say about flying a helicopter:

"The thing is, helicopters are different from planes. An airplane by its nature wants to fly, and if not interfered with too strongly by unusual events or by an incompetent pilot, it will fly. A helicopter does not want to fly. It is maintained in the air by a variety of forces and controls working in opposition to each other. Having said all this, I must admit that flying in a helicopter is one of the most satisfying and exhilarating experiences I have ever enjoyed: skimming over the tops of trees at 100 knots is something we should all be able to do, at least once".

It's not easy, but once you get the hang of it—it's a thrill beyond words. My flight instructor, Damien, had to have enough faith in me to give me the controls and let me fly the thing. Then he had to have enough faith in me to get out of the cockpit and tell me it was time for me to solo. I've never sweated so much in my life. But I did it. My flight instructor had enough faith in me to give me a quarter-of-a-million dollar machine and tell me to bring it (and me!) back in one piece. Another gift—thanks, Damien.

And the list goes on and on. How about you? How many names have you added to your list? What do you say we take a break? I'll stop typing and you stop reading. We'll both pick up the phone, send out an e-mail, or use the good old fashion post office to tell at least one person from our list (the list of names of the people who had faith in us) how much we appreciated their trust, their time, and their patience. We should probably do it now. Some of the most influential people in my life are dead, so I can't thank them. I'm not gonna wait until I deliver a eulogy at their funeral to let them know how much they mean to me.

can i get there from here?

Didn't that feel great! Why is it we wait until people are gone before we share memories of them and the impact they had on our lives? If these good, influential people mean so much to us, why do we wait until the viewing or funeral to let their families know it? Another thing in life that leaves me scratching my head. Kinda like: Why do we *truck* a *ship*ment; but *ship cargo*? The things that keep me up at night...

Another thing that keeps me up at night—my fiancée (go ahead and add 10 points for that, she's worth it!). Yep, my story ends here with the angel in my life. Actually, this is where my life begins.

We plan to get married in the next couple of months. Hopefully my dogs will get along with her dog *and* cats, and my children will adjust to everyone living together. In order to get to this point, I have to back-track a little bit. I know, another tangent, another story, another... Just bear with me, it'll all make sense—trust me.

Quick synopsis: I was married in the early eighties. This contentious relationship turned into an unhealthy relationship, but two boys were born from the marriage—both remarkable young men. I took helicopter lessons, like I said earlier, because I always wanted to learn to fly and we had the money for me to try it. I completed all my flight time, passed the written test (with a ninety-two—thank you very much), and had my check ride date set with the FAA flight examiner. One week before my check ride—the ride that would give me my private pilot's license—I was rushed to the hospital with chest pains. I wasn't having a heart attack at that time, as the tests would show. But the tests did show an old heart attack sometime in my past. One that I never knew I had. That took care of flying.

But it opened my eyes to what stress can do to the body. Stress is a *very powerful* force in our lives. I had no family history, no risk factors, no lifestyle factors, and my blood work was "stone cold perfect" according to my cardiologist. So what caused the heart attack? S-t-r-e-s-s. I didn't sleep very well that night in the hospital, so I did a lot of thinking.

Long and short of it: separation, divorce, trying to find a place to live. And then it happens. Out of nowhere an angel appears. Mine was in the form of a beautiful woman who would prove to have faith in me beyond my wildest dreams. She made sure I had a house to raise my boys in and then she made sure I didn't give up on myself.

We would always pass by a small community church while running our daily errands. It is the only church in town. My angel began dialogues of faith, believing, worship, and those sorts of things. I didn't want to disappoint her, so I went along with the conversations. She mentioned more than once that she wanted to go to a service at this little community church.

Again, not wanting to disappoint her, I came up with excuse after excuse each Sunday morning. And I thought I was doing pretty good for a while until she called me and told me she was picking me up, to be ready by nine. I don't know who I was more scared for: me or the rest of the congregation in the church. I was sure lightning was going to strike when I walked through the doors. But you know something? Somehow I made it through the service and I found myself

can i get there from here?

walking out of there feeling at peace with myself. For the first time in a long time, I was at peace.

There were no revelations that would make this start of my *new* faith any more exciting; no epiphanies that would make you wonder why it didn't happen to you, and no magical signs that made me believe again. Nope, as subtle and quietly as I entered those doors, just as subtle was the transformation. It's amazing what an open heart can do! We've been going to church together every Sunday now and we are getting involved with other church activities, which keeps us busy. Why? I guess we're getting too old to go to the bars and dance all night!

Here's why I call her an angel—something wonderful—if you will. The chances of us meeting had to be slim. Like any relationship, forces have to come into play to make people meet. She had the opportunity to become an administrator at another school, but it didn't work out. There were three high schools that needed resource officers and three of us had the training. I just happened to be assigned to the same school where she was teaching. She got in a minor accident and needed a police report. Years went by and we became friends. After I was separated, I begin joking with her about us "getting together." She took a chance on me after I got divorced and things got better each day.

What were the chances? All of those things had to happen, in the order they did, for us to meet and become friends. What would the chances be that my new house would be right down the street from our church—making us pass by the church regularly? I could have found a house anywhere. And for her to bring me—drag me—to church that Sunday morning…

She has faith in me like no one else has ever had. Wanna

know who's behind the writing of this book? Wanna know who's behind me now, proceeding with becoming an ordained minister? Yep, something I wanted 30 years ago is actually going to happen. I don't know why it took this long, but there must have been a reason. Someone who has faith in you; that person is a gift. Someone this special having faith in you is something else. I wish I could say it better, but it's just something else.

Her name—Elissa. Elissa has become my rock and my foundation. I know I don't deserve her, but I'm not gonna turn this down. Something like this (our relationship) only comes along once in a lifetime.

So why did I tell you about her? To make you jealous! I have her and you don't—it's that simple. Nah, actually I was going to make a point about life. If thirty or so years ago someone was to tell me that in order for me to get to this point in my life—raising my two boys, engaged to a phenomenal woman, being happier than I've ever been in my life—that I would have to endure my past, then I would have told them to forget it. I set out to become a priest, and ended up a cop. Had someone told me I would have to undergo what I have so far in life just to be the person I am today, I'd tell them to go pound sand. Just in the past twenty or so years, I've endured a volatile relationship, suffered a traumatic brain injury (another story for another book), gone through the hell that is divorce, experienced custody and child support disputes, moved from a house (I rebuilt it myself) into an apartment, moved again six months later into a house that's fifty years old (and shows it), lost most of everything in the divorce that I've worked for, and lived paycheck to paycheck in order to raise two children on my own.

No way would I take on the life that was to become mine. I just wouldn't agree to it! Have you ever looked back and wondered, if you could: would I go back and change a part of my life? There's no way I could have predicted *or* accepted that this would be the way my life would turn out. But you know what? I wouldn't have it any other way! Looking back now, I endured the hardships for a reason. Those hardships made me who I am today. They could have been roadblocks, but they ended up being hurdles (sound familiar?). I could never have had the thoughts for this book without the life that I lived. I could never be the father I am today if I didn't live the life that I lived. And I could have never met and fallen in love with an angel without living the life I lived.

I'm sure there were signs along the road—my life—that pointed in this direction. Looking back, I know there was a purpose to my life. The ultimate traffic engineer laid out this road for me. I did the driving and I made the decisions, but he laid it out. Another gift from the ultimate gift-giver. Anyone else feel like that? Has your life been outlined for you to travel to a destination that is still largely unknown? Isn't it hard to not try and figure out where we're going instead of enjoying the scenery of the trip? Could our faith in the trip itself be another gift?

And speaking of gifts, do you remember the GPS system *I didn't get* for Christmas? What if faith was our GPS navigation system? Can you imagine being anywhere and never being lost? Our GPS system would guide us safely to where we wanted to go—to our destination. And it would also tell us where we are.

Imagine if we were lost in an unknown neighborhood—

maybe a really bad one in a city we're visiting. We made a wrong turn, and because we guys never want to admit we're wrong, we never ask for directions. We find ourselves in a dangerous situation with no idea how to get out of it. Sound like anyone's life? Anyway, we're able to remain calm because we know we can count on our GPS navigation system (our faith) to tell us where we are. And once we know where we are, isn't it easier to find our way back?

Remember, this unbelievable device not only tells us where we are, but it also tells us how to get to where we want to go—our destination. Maybe that destination is contentment; maybe it's a level of understanding we want to achieve; perhaps it's love or kindness or gentleness; or maybe it's even getting to know God. Imagine a system that requires you to do nothing more than plug it in and turn it on. Maybe that's like faith.

We get in our car and drive down the superhighway of life. The signs are there telling us our location, and the information and exit signs are programmed into our GPS. If we take a look at the manual—maybe like the Bible—we have a better understanding of our device (our faith). Once we know how it works and understand and trust it, we head out to explore. We now have more trust in our car (our life) because of this little device; we have more trust in our route of travel (our decisions) because of this little device, and we have confidence (assurance) we'll get to where we want to go because of this little device. And what can we call our little device—*faith*.

What a gift! The gift of faith. It's always the right size, the right color, and it's never out of style. You don't need a receipt to worry about taking it back to the store, and it's yours to keep forever. It's been given to you unconditionally and without cost—the giver of the gift paid the ultimate price for it. You can use it whenever you want, however many times you want, and it never loses power. That is, unless you decide to unplug it. Even if you throw it around and don't take the proper care of it, it'll still work the next time you plug it in. Maybe we should call faith the indestructible gift.

That's one analogy for faith that comes to mind. If you paid attention and were keeping score, there were other analogies for faith throughout this book. Some were subtle and some not so subtle. But they were placed there along the way to get us to think about things in a different light. I've learned that sometimes the best way to learn is to not know you're actually learning while you're learning. Go ahead; try to argue with that logic! But think about it, aren't there times when you've remembered something that made no sense when you first heard it, then later you remembered the message of what was said? Now you're beginning to understand the madness that is my brain...

If this book crammed religion and faith and worship down your throat, how far would you have gotten? I bet not this far. Instead it was written with the intent to offer subtle reminders of how lucky we are to be alive and have a loving God who has faith in us. Kind of like the way I felt while in church for the first time in years. Our ministers are the most open, warm, and friendly preachers Elissa and I have ever met. They're approachable, and they made us feel at home from the first time we entered the church. Without them, I wouldn't have gotten to this place in my life. So it's with appreciation that I say thank you to Steve, Ginny, and

Andrew. You are truly doing God's work and for all you have given to Elissa and me, and everyone else. *Thank You*!

Steve, Ginny, and Andrew are like beacons of light on a dark, cloudy day. They shine brightly. And that reminds me of a story told by Dwight Moody. It's a short story:

> *A blind man was sitting on a street corner in a large city holding a lantern. One day a passerby stopped and asked the blind man why he held the lantern because the light of it was of no use to him—he was blind. The blind man simply replied, "so that others won't stumble."*

What a concept, holding up a lantern so others won't stumble. How many of us hold up a lantern to ensure others won't stumble? Who's holding up a lantern for us? Didn't I read somewhere that Jesus said, "I am the light"? What a great source of hope— our Lord is our light. And if he is the light, what is our faith?

How many references have I made about batteries for my flashlight (10 more points your way if you know it)? What if God (and by default, Jesus) really is our flashlight—nearby, ready for us whenever we need it (er, Him)? The bulb is always fresh, and it's waterproof and unbreakable. All we need to do is insert the batteries—*our faith*—to make it burn brightly. That would be something. And isn't that a lot like what we're talking about here? The flashlight is always there; always on the ready—whenever we need it to light the way. And it's when we're in darkness that we need it the most.

Have you ever searched for batteries in the pitch dark? Like when a storm rolls in and the power goes out. Wouldn't it be smart to look for the batteries and make sure they're in the flashlight before the storm hits? Aren't we all either in a storm, coming out of a storm, or heading into a storm? Face it, storms are part of our lives, so why not be prepared? Maybe the time to insert our batteries (our faith) into our flashlights (our Lord) is before we're in the dark. That's the time when we have a clear head and we can think straight; not when the power is out and panic is setting in as we frantically search for the batteries. If we put our batteries in before we need the light, all we have to do is turn the flashlight on. We can count on our batteries (faith) being there.

I know I have cursed at my light for not working when I needed it the most. What if I had taken a little time before I needed the flashlight and made sure the batteries were in? I would have avoided a lot of anxiety, even anger, at my flashlight.

What about rechargeable batteries, you ask. Great question—here's how they get recharged: church. Yep, a once-a-week dose of church will recharge those batteries so they're there for you the rest of the week.

"But I don't have time to go to church; does that mean the batteries won't work?" They'll work, but maybe your light won't shine as bright as it used to ...

Here's something about these two analogies—a GPS navigation system and a flashlight—that makes me scratch my head *again*: Why do we trust these devices so much? We've come such a long way in the development of the technology that makes our lives better. Who would have thought twenty years ago that you could plug a small device into your cigarette lighter and the thing would tell you (literally) how to get anywhere you wanted to go. And that it would even have detour routes built into it in the event you encountered one. And who would have thought flashlights could be half the size they were twenty years ago, yet be ten times more powerful.

We use these electronic devices without a second thought. We trust that they were built to the standards we're accustomed to. And we assume that they'll work whenever we need them. Some of us have actually put our lives in their hands. That is, put our trust—our blind faith—into these devices to either save our butts or make sure we were safe. Personally speaking (as a cop); having a working flashlight on night-watch will literally save your life.

Walking up to a car at two thirty in the morning—not knowing who is in the car or what the occupants are holding—is one of the most dangerous parts of police work. When a cop walks up to a car that he's just pulled over, he has no idea what lies in store for him. He knows it could very well be the last car stop he ever makes. And yet, he places his life in the hands of the flashlight he's holding to illuminate the inside of the car to see just who he's dealing with and what they might be hiding. The cop doesn't think twice about pushing the button and assuming the light will work—the light will ensure he sees what he's getting into.

As far as the GPS, have you ever been a couple thousand feet in the air and had no idea where you were? That's *not* a good feeling, trust me. As a student pilot, I knew I could glance at my GPS unit, and it would show me exactly where I was, whose airspace I was in, if I was getting close (make that *too close*) to a restricted military zone, even where the nearest airport was. It would also track my route, and it could actually calculate what time I would arrive at my destination, how much fuel I would have in reserve, and make corrections for wind direction

can i get there from here?

and velocity. Now that's a handy piece of equipment to have if you find yourself on the wrong side of the clouds!

That's just two examples. How many other electronic gadgets do we trust our lives with? I bet you can think of a few I didn't come up with. So here's my point: why do we put so much *faith* in these devices without thinking twice about them? Yet, when it comes to having faith in something we *know* to be the truth, we have problems? Do we honestly have more faith in the assembly workers who put these things together than we do in our God?

Speaking of faith, what about this saying: *a computer is only as smart as the person who programmed it*. Have any of us ever thought about what kind of day the person on the assembly line, in a country halfway around the world, might be having? Some anonymous someone is putting our gadgets/devices/tools together. We don't know what kind of integrity they have, we don't know what values they have, and we certainly don't know what kind of person(s) they are. If they don't know us, do they really care about us? Do they think, as they assemble the gadgets/devices/tools they're responsible for: "I'm building this—putting it together—for *you*?" Can they even think about each and every one of us who are on the other end buying them? No way. And that doesn't mean they aren't good people; it's just that they have a job to do and that means building so many of these things each shift. There's no way they have time to think about each individual person who will eventually purchase *and* use them.

We haven't thought about that and it doesn't mean we should go into panic mode either. It's just that if we're able to have trust and faith in these devices, why can't we find that same trust and faith in God? It seems to reason that since God loves us, knows each and every one of us by name, gave his Son to us for our salvation, and promised us our own little piece of heaven, he might be the one whom we should trust with our faith. Having faith in a piece of electronics is nice, but having faith in *The One* who will provide everything we will ever need—for eternity—is something altogether different.

Well, that's just the way I'm looking at this. Maybe I'm the crazy one; maybe I should trust that my GPS system (if I ever get one) and my flashlight will work for me every time I need them. Perhaps I should re-think my position on who has my best interests at heart while I'm using them.

Ya know what? I tried that route for too many years. As I look back, I don't see fulfillment; I see a lot of emptiness, a lot of missed opportunities, and a lot of wrong turns and being lost—as well as being in the dark on a lot of things I thought I knew. If only I had a navigation system and flashlight to guide me and light the way...

Sometimes it takes a life-changing event to get us to *have faith again* (or *wake up and smell the coffee*, as my dad used to say). If that's what you're waiting for—a tragic event—good luck. I hope something tragic happens in your life so that you're able to feel the Lord's love. Are you out of your mind? A tragedy has gotta be one of the most insensitive and cruel things anyone could wish on another person. But isn't that what we sometimes do to ourselves? We wait until something bad happens—almost anticipating something bad happening—before we act.

Like me going back to church. I don't know what I was

waiting for, but I was waiting for something—some reason, some excuse, some kind of motivation to get me to take that first step. I don't know why, but it was almost as if I was telling myself that if I had a reason to restore my faith, then I'd look in that direction. We've already talked about what the reasons are that we talk to God. And didn't we agree earlier that for the most part, it usually takes something bad for us to open a dialogue with God?

How about if we agree to not wait for something to happen? What do you say we go after life with gusto and with a sense of joy instead of being a spectator? No one wants to wish anything bad on another person; well, most of us anyway. Instead of hoping you get some sort of sign from God that says it's time to reconnect with him. I'm gonna hope and pray that you make the decision now to do whatever is necessary to enjoy life. And if you already have a fantastic relationship with God, then my hope and prayers are for you to continue a fulfilled life with purpose and joy.

Enjoyment, fulfillment, purpose, and joy. Four words from the previous paragraph that, if we choose, can surround our faith like spokes in a wheel. Faith can serve *enjoyment* in life; faith can serve *fulfillment* in life; faith can serve *purpose* in life, and faith can serve *joy* in life.

Enjoyment, fulfillment, purpose, and joy. This book is the product of the sum of my two boys, Matt and Corey, who have brought me back to having faith in myself. It's both rewarding and scary as hell to have two lives who have invested their faith in you and your beliefs, values, and morals. Add to that an angel, and well...now I think I got it made!

But these three have given me the strength to write, re-write, modify, and edit by asking me day in and day out how I was doing with the book. They read parts of it, sometimes laughing and other times asking questions. But the whole time, they had faith in me. What a gift, the three most important people in your life having faith in you.

Faith has served me well, and my hope and prayer is that it has and will continue to serve you. And with hope and prayer and faith, anything is possible. Like this book being finished!

epilogue

Encarta Dictionary: ep-i-logue (noun)

A short chapter or section at the end of a literary work, sometimes detailing the fate of its characters.

First of all, I can't believe that I could ever produce a piece of *literary work*. Nah, if I went back some years ago and thought this would be possible, I'd say to myself, "no way." But apparently faith has intervened, and here it is.

Does anyone remember the 1970s TV show, *The F.B.I.*? I can remember my dad letting us stay up late to watch it on Sunday nights. It opened with the announcer saying: "The F-B-I, starring Efrem Zimbalist, Jr." And it had a further announcement that it was *in color*. Those were the days, weren't they? A TV show in color—and I was my dad's personal remote control! The show had four acts, and they were divided for the commercial breaks. The word *Act I* would be shown on the screen, then the action, and then there would be the first set of commercials; next *Act II*, the second set of

can i get there from here?

commercials; then *Act III* and *IV* in that order. Around five minutes before nine o'clock, *Epilogue* would be displayed on the screen, and the show would summarize what the bad guys were found guilty of and how many years they got. It seemed like every suspect charged was found guilty of Interstate Flight to Avoid Prosecution in the *Epilogue*.

That's what this part of the book is about. No, not what we've been found guilty of—Interstate Flight to Avoid Prosecution. Instead it's a wrap-up of everything we've discussed. Teachers call it a summary. They sum-up a lesson to make sure the students understand the concept of what was presented in their class. Others might call it a conclusion (I know my science teachers would be proud that I remembered the scientific method).

So here it is; the conclusion, summary, or epilogue—take your pick on which term you prefer. Since we began our journey—introduced a hypothesis—in the first pages of this book, we learned together and agreed that:

- There is a God, who is a loving God.
- God knows each and every one of us as his children.
- Jesus lived knowing his entire life that he would be crucified.
- God sent Jesus, his only Son, to us for our salvation—our eternal life.
- The Bible is an accurate historic book detailing God's love for us as well as the life of his Son, Jesus Christ.
- There are miracles, signs from God, happening all around us—it's up to us to see and appreciate them.

- Bad things happen to good people because God loves us enough to give us free will.
- When we're searching for answers, we should start with God and go from there.
- We have all doubted our faith—whether in God or someone else—at one time or another.
- It's amazing to think of the faith that others have had in us.
- Finding faith in God and in ourselves is easier than we thought—if we just keep it simple.

The definition of epilogue ends with: "...detailing the *fate* of its *characters*."

As far as the character thing goes, perhaps we're all characters—each and every one of us is a character who we've read about.

As far as our fate, that's our own individual book to write, our own personal journey down life's superhighway. But with faith, we know we're not going it alone.

Hey, I almost forgot...It's now November–2008. Boy how time flies! Yep, it took all that time from when I started this until now when it's really gonna get published. I thought I'd fill you in on a few things that happened since you opened the first pages of this book. Hopefully it didn't take you a year to read it, like it took me to get here. But if it did, welcome to the club. I told you we were a lot alike; me and you.

First and foremost, I married my angel! Last Father's Day we got married in our church and had a small reception following the ceremony. My kids set us up at the reception by having us stand in front of the cake for a picture. As the picture was about to be taken, they hit us both in the face with pieces of the cake that had already been cut. I tried telling Elissa that I came with baggage, but she just wouldn't listen!

Boomer's been chasing the cats around the house and eating their food. Bojangles (the cat) has given him a couple of good swats across his nose, but that hasn't stopped him. I lost count of how many things have been broken with all the running around they do. Boomer and Buck (my other dog) sleep wherever thy want and their hair is everywhere, especially on the couch and in the bed. Elissa's dog is a cute little Tibetan Terrier named Bosco. She doesn't like Boomer, even a little bit; probably because he steals her food whenever she's not looking. This little 20 pound fur-ball has gone after him more times than I can recall. She isn't taking any of his crap and she lets him know it! Buck and Bojangles run after each other, knocking more of Elissa's antiques to the floor and my kids have made themselves at home the only way a 16 and a 20 year old know how to do. I think you get the picture. Again, I told her I came with baggage.

And after a short 28 year hiatus from school, I was able to re-focus and fulfill a dream my parents had for me more than three decades ago. I finished my bachelor's degree in Christian counseling. Yeah, I hear you; this guy's gonna be talking to people and giving them advice! Another one of life's mysteries.

One more thing: You can now call me Reverend Rusty Williams! Can you believe that? I just received my ordination and am now officially an ordained minister. I told you this thing called life was crazy. I kept looking up and shaking my head no, but *He* just wouldn't take no for an answer.

I guess he has more faith in me than I realize. Kinda makes ya wonder, doesn't it?

So there you have it, questions that we were able to answer, which hopefully brought us closer to understanding the potential of our faith. What do you say we pop some batteries in our flashlights, plug in our GPS system, and see where our roads lead—without forgetting to enjoy the scenery along the way.

Maybe our paths will cross someday and we can compare notes.

Until then...

For my brothers and sisters in law enforcement:

> *"Blessed are the peacemakers, for they shall be called sons of God"*
>
> Matthew 5:9

And don't forget to laugh!
　　Especially At Yourself.
　　When you're laughing at yourself more than you're laughing at others, that's when you know you're gonna be fine.

P.S. If you were keeping score throughout the book, forget about it—the points never counted. Isn't that a lot like life? We all want to keep score, but in the end it really doesn't matter.

Contact the author at
www.CanIGetThere.com
Or
Rusty Williams
P.O. Box 2235
Medford Lakes, NJ
08055